A PERSONAL LEADERSHIP
Guide FOR
YOUTH

NTANGEKI NSHALA

A PERSONAL LEADERSHIP
Guide FOR
YOUTH

50 IMPORTANT LIFE SKILLS NEVER TAUGHT IN **SCHOOL**

ii

REVIEWS

"One of the most powerful books I have ever read. A deserving companion to every youth"
- **Dr. Hawa Mkwela,**
  Parent

"The book is a wow! A fantastic teacher on the move, for upcoming (young) leaders. It is energizing, inspirational and a leader's coach."
- **Dr. Sabetha James Mwambenja,**
  Managing Director - Covenant Bank for Women.

The book, to say the least, is inspiring, andmotivating. It has a broad spectrum of useful life's material. I believe it to be an easy reading book for all youth, and an enlightening extracurricular reading for all.
- **Mary H.C.S Longway,**
  Judge of the High Court (Rtd)

"This book is a road map for our youth today; a road map towards one of the highest human aspirations and ambition; that is to be a good person. A person with both a willingness and ability to combine academic competency with a deep concern for moral and spiritual values. It challenges our youth to always seek faith, knowledge and truth as a unity and encourages them to commit themselves in the development of skills for life-long learning, an ethic of care and a genuine desire for excellence in all areas of their life.

Developing a set of moral standard does not happen by miracle, magic or luck. It happens through hard work and determination, tests and victories throughout life. Though some values are taught within subjects in schools at various levels, and in general, teachers in most academic institutions take advantage of any teachable moment that arise unexpectedly, both parents and educators are acutely aware that values such as respect, tolerance, love, confidence, courage, humility, discipline, honesty and responsibility have to be taught formally and informally in schools and especially at home precisely because not everything can be taught in school.

This book will, undoubtedly, inspire our youth to always better themselves by finding a new path, a new direction in which they will be at their very best."
– **Fr. Gaudence Mushi CSSP,**
   Libermann Boy' s Secondary School.

A PERSONAL LEADERSHIP *Guide* FOR YOUTH

50 Important Life Skills Never Taught in School

NTANGEKI NSHALLA

Ntangeki Nshala

Published by Ntangeki Nshala
Mazinde/Ruvu Street, Plot no. 129, Block A
P. O. Box 79430, Dar es Salaam, Tanzania.
Email: ntangeki@ntangekinshala.com

Personal Leadership for Youth
@Ntangeki Nshala, 2017
All Rights Reserved.
ISBN: 978-9976-89-601-5

All rights reserved. No part of this publication may be reproduced, stored in a retrieval system, or transmitted, in any form or by any means, mechanical, photocopying, recording or otherwise, without prior written permission of the publisher.

Designed by Lillian R. Kessy

Printed by Thomson Press (I) Ltd, Faridabad (Harynana)

Ntangeki Nshala

DEDICATION

To my Mother, Ma Anthonia Alexander Kajumulo for her love and tireless support.

— *Ntangeki Nshala* —

"Good habits formed at Youth makes all the difference"

x

TABLE OF CONTENTS

1. Born to Lead 7
2. Fear of God 11
3. Dream Big 15
4. Parent's Pride 18
5. Finish Your Greens 22
6. Home Alone 25
7. Smart & Clean 29
8. Eagles Flock with Eagles 32
9. Read Read Read! 35
10. Sit in Front 39
11. Volunteer to Lead 43
12. Family First 46
13. Fear Fear! 50
14. Time is Precious 54
15. Stand the Peer Pressure 57
16. Girls Power 60
17. Boys to Men 64

18.	Truth will Set You Free	67
19.	Devil's Workshop	70
20.	Work Hard	74
21.	A Myth of a Private Life	78
22.	Hired for Attitude	82
23.	Sky is Never the Limit	86
24.	Never Lose Your Cool	89
25.	Think	92
26.	Critical Thinking	96
27.	Dig Gold Where You Are	99
28.	Biija Mpola	103
29.	In Rome, Be a Roman	107
30.	Education is Key	111
31.	Talent is Never Enough	115
32.	Kindness Matters	119
33.	Exercise is Power	123
34.	Live Legally	127
35.	Set Goals	131
36.	Fluent in Finance	136
37.	A Wolf in a Pack	141

38.	The Power of Words	145
39.	Who is Your Role Model	149
40.	A Drop of Greatness	153
41.	Laugh out Loud	157
42.	Howl Like a Wolf	161
43.	The Spirit of Charity	165
44.	Floor Your Flaws	169
45.	Excellence	173
46.	Be Like MJ	177
47.	Keep Your Word	181
48.	Be Humble	185
49.	A Valuable Brand	189
50.	It's Show Time	193

— *Ntangeki Nshala* —

FOREWORD

From the first glance I saw Ntangeki when he visited my office I saw a unique thing in him. The way he was talking about his passion into inspirational talks, public speaking as well as authorship, something that I was also doing, the fire in him made me trust what I was expecting and with no time I have seen the result after holding his second book in my hands. Sincerely, this kind of passion and commitment is rarely to find in many Tanzanian young men and women of his age.

After our frequent meetings and conversation I came to know Ntangeki Nshala as an accountant, a banker who has moved his way out from employment to entrepreneurship, he is now a wonderful author and an inspirational speaker. Still I see many rivers that will continue to flow out of him to feed the hungry world.

Allow me to be a witness to you after reading with peace of work. Personal Leadership for Youth is a book that everyone needs to read. Yes it is written for youth but I am sure every parent needs to read first and see the valuable materials inside it before you recommend your son or daughter to read. If you will just buy it for your

Ntangeki Nshala

child without reading it you will not explain to him/her with the required weight on the importance of reading and finishing it, by the way when I was reading this book as a parent it was like a mirror showing me important things that many parents forget to share with their children. This book will give you parent a wonderful self-reflection, it will guide youths in very important areas of life so as to pave their ways to success.

The quality of this book is commendable and of international standards. It carries 50 important life skills that are not frequently taught in our conventional schools but very remarkable skills in everyday life. These skills ranges from personal development, dealing with fear, the value of trying more and more, the value of faith, healthy tips as well as valuing family and parents. It is not an academic book but sincerely it contain more than what academics can offer you. The language is simple for every person to understand. I love the way the author have tried to mix very relevant sayings and quotes from famous authors, leaders and former remarkable individuals to support the message of the book. This is a book that once you start a page, it is hard to stop.

Being a teacher as primary lever, secondary lever and currently a university lecturer, I have encounter hundreds of youths who are so passionately with their future and dreams but unfortunately lacking some valuable life skills necessary for their journey.I am happy to announce that the missed skills are now at your fingertips. Make this book your daily guide and you will see the results.

Dr. Chris Mauki PhD
University of Dar es Salaam

— *Ntangeki Nshala* —

PREFACE

Mid 2016 after I had completed the draft for my first title, *Your Personal Leadership Guide*, I was excited and looking forward to have my first book on the shelves of bookstores which I frequently visit.

One Saturday mid morning, while alone in my office, I was meditating and a new idea knocked on my mind. It was about my next book project. While I knew my first book would suite a wide range of readers; from youth in schools, managers, senior executives, CEOs and entrepreneurs, I still thought there was one group that would struggle to understand it fully. The youth.

This made me recall my memories in secondary school, high school and college and figure out what would have been an ideal book that I would have enjoyed back then. At the same time having gone through life until now, as a father, former corporate executive and an entrepreneur, what would be the right message that would supplement what our youth are taught in schools and colleges.

Since my life purpose is to unlock people's leadership potential, I received this new idea with great pleasure, believing it must be a message from Above. I believe the Holy Spirit wanted me to touch these young lives and prepare them for a complex future.

I immediately began to study it and see how best I could present the message so that it can be acceptable and useful. It has been a challenge to find a voice that can resonate with the youth, but I am glad that I finally found it and hope it will be in unison with a many youth around the world.

I have enjoyed every bit of this journey, and I hope that through this book, many lives will be changed, great results will be achieved and individuals, families, communities, nations and the world will become better.

I was surprised by the feedback that I received from my friend Dr. Hawa Mkwela, who was the first person to read the draft other than myself. She said that this book will be very useful not only to our children, but parents as well. She said this book will be a valuable tool for parenting. In here, parents are reminded of the important habits they are supposed to teach their children, and they also will learn about new valuable areas that they might not have thought about.

In that regard this book now becomes a useful tool for the whole family. It will assist parents in parenting and at the same time guide their youth in improving their self awareness and personal leadership.

It is my wish and prayer that this book will challenge our youth not to be comfortable with the predictability of yesterday, but be ready for the realities of today and prepare for the unknown challenges of tomorrow.

Ntangeki Nshala

ntangeki@ntangekinshala.com

Ntangeki Nshala

ACKNOWLEDGEMENT

I would like put forward my sincerely appreciation to Dr. Hawa Mkwela for reading the draft and offering useful thoughts.

Thanks to my children, Ishengoma, Nyakato and Kiiza for being the source of happiness and making my life meaningful.

But above all special thanks to my wife, Theodosia for her immeasurable love and invaluable support.

INTRODUCTION

If I were to summarize this book in three words then the best words would be, "Catch Them Young."

This book, *A Personal Leadership Guide for Youth, 50 Important Life Skills Never Taught in School,* is all about preparing our youth for the tough life ahead of them. It aims at preparing the youth for a 21st century life, a fast changing life full of uncertainties and possibilities, challenges and opportunities, ups and downs, triumphs and disappointments.

I have written this book after having gone through life and found out that the good performance in formal education alone does not guarantee success in life. Naturally, the greatest wish of a parent is to guide and help his or her child grow up to become a successful person, a good citizen, a caring spouse and a loving parent too. But to the disappointment of many parents, hopes for their children have gone astray after spending a lot of efforts on formal education.

There is no doubt that formal education is very important, but success requires much more than that. That is why our communities are filled with many graduates who cannot find a job. How many times have we come across people who were the best in class but are struggling to be promoted at work? Or in the corporate world where young officers climb the ladder much faster leaving behind people who were there for years. This is the reality of life and that is why I want your child to be molded from early on. To be prepared for the challenges around them and be on the winning side in future.

The 50 important life skills never taught in school are really important. They touch on many aspects of a normal life and most of the times they seem to be common sense, but are normally not a common practice.

In this book you will learn the importance of self awareness, appreciate the importance of taking your life into your own hands, following your life's dream and work hard to accomplish it. When the dream is clear, then you will need to plan and put down goals that will keep you on track.

The largest part of this book is about the mind work. Preparing you by building character that is the vehicle for success. If I take an example of a vehicle, then your formal education can be the engine. Very important. But engine alone cannot move the vehicle. You need wheels, fuels, electric system, brakes, and many other parts. Now these parts are honesty, confidence, hard work, attitude, physical health, discipline, kindness, emotional intelligence, focus, patience and so on.

All these and many others have been discussed in a manner that will easily be understood by the youth and can be embraced and practiced in any environment. This is not an academic book so the language used is expected to be simple, motivating and examples used are likely to inspire change.

21st century is the most exciting time to live in. It is in this period the world has become more linked and opportunities become more global. Communication is a lot easier, efficient and cheap, while movements have become smoother than ever before. There is more freedom for one to be whoever they want to become, and possibilities are unlimited. If there is anything that can stop you from living your dream, that thing will be yourself.

Please, don't fail yourself, prepare now for your dream life.

Ntangeki Nshala

A PERSONAL LEADERSHIP
Guide FOR
YOUTH

1

Born to Lead

October 2016 I was invited to speak at one of the UNESCO Youth programs run in various colleges, and this time it was at The Institute of Finance Management, (IFM) in Dar es Salaam. It was an audience of more than 300 students most from IFM and a few other colleges. I started my speech by asking all leaders in the room to put up their hands. Only a handful did. If you were in the crowd as well, would you have raised your hand or not?
Well, I have news for you. You are a leader too. Don't tell me you are not because you do not have a title, or because no one is under your command, or you are not a class monitor, or prefect, or not in charge of any group. Fine, you may not be all that, but you are still a leader. A leader without a title as Robin Sharma would put it.

The fact of life is that everyone is a leader because every human being is born with the capability and responsibility to lead. The first person that you lead is yourself.

You might now be asking yourself, how are you a leader and what have you done to show that you are leading. As I said, you do not have to have a crowd behind you, most people have the audience of one.

When you are living at home with parents or when you at school under teachers, you might not notice your role in leading yourself. But if you look carefully you will note that many times your parents will ask you about the things that you prefer. They will ask you about food, clothes, toys, places to go, the school you prefer, the colleges you want to go to, the career you want to have and so on. The moment you start selecting one choice over another that is the moment your personal leadership starts.

Your parents start training you on leading yourself from a very young age, but most of the time we do not realize it. Parents like to see their children grow up and build the capability to lead themselves. This is because although parents brought us into this world, everyone has their own life. Parents have their own life and so do you. However much they love you, they cannot live for you. You are on your own, and parents can only assist that much.

Born to Lead

The earlier you realize that you are on your own, and your future depends on you, not anyone else, the better.

If you are in school or college, teachers are there to assist you to learn so that you can become who you dream to be. They are not there to push you, or punish you or terrorize you and force you to study, not at all. They are there to assist. For this reason from today, you need to look at your teachers differently. They are your friends. They want you to succeed, and they celebrate when you do.

Like parents, teachers can only do so much, and the rest will depend on you. At this point, the difference between good leaders and poor leaders starts to be clear. Those good leaders will lead themselves into studying hard, being punctual, appearing smart and clean, being honest and trustworthy. Good leaders will obey school and college rules, will be focused on their studies and will avoid bad influences. Good leaders will always reach their dreams because they choose to lead themselves towards them. That is what I call personal leadership.

Poor leaders will always wait to be pushed to do things, they will not focus on important activities, like their studies, but will always engage in useless short-lived pleasures like going out and parties. Poor leaders will seek to show off their beauty and wealth, will spend their parent's money on useless expenditures and will not respect their teachers or rules. A poor leader will never be given any role as leaders at school or college. Definitely, a poor leader will have poor results and will not reach his or her dreams. All these are personal choices, it is personal leadership.

Jack Ma, one of the world's most successful businessman, once said, "If you are born poor, it is not your fault, but if you die poor it is your fault." I also say, if you fail to succeed in your life, it is not because of your parents, or teachers, it is 100% your fault.

Start now and take your life in your hands. Know that parents and teachers are there to assist, but success or failure is your personal business.

The fact of life is that everyone is a leader because every human being is born with the capability and responsibility to lead. The first person that you lead is yourself.

2

Fear of God

Last Sunday, as we sat around the dining table for lunch, my wife and I started to pray for the food we were about to have. In the middle of the prayer, we could not help ourselves from smiling as both of us looked at our son, Kiiza, who also joined us and seeing us pray, he also humbled himself and did a rough sign of the cross. Kiiza just turned two years, but the way he behaved is as though he understood everything we said.

It is amazing how children learn. They are very sharp in observing all movements grownups make and do exactly the same. That is why it is said the best time to plant the life principals in a child is from birth to the age of twelve. Researchers have proven that this is the age period children take in all that they see and hear.

Therefore as parents, my wife and I have taken it upon ourselves to instill all good principals of personal leadership in our children during this period. The smile we exchanged when Kiiza prayed with us at the dining table was a confirmation to us that we are on track, and it is working.

I presume that as a young boy or girl, your parents must have taken you through the same training. It is the first training all youth need to go through. You have to know God and fear Him because He is the Almighty.

Yes, I said, Fear Him, but not to be scared of Him. Fear of God means to have reverence (great respect) for Him knowing that He is the beginning and the end of your life.

Have faith, believe in Him, knowing that He has the power to help you in whatever you wish to be. If you live according to His commandments, your life will be filled with His blessings and success. In that case, you have to know what and how God wants you to live your life and that in the end, when you depart from this world, will join His eternal life. At the same time if you live in a manner that does not please Him, your material success will not generate true happiness in your life.

In the fear of the LORD there is strong confidence, and his children will have refuge. The fear of the LORD is a fountain of life, that one may avoid the snares of death - Proverbs 14:26-27

Fear of God

So from a young age, you have to know how to live in a manner that manifests fear of God in you. You have to learn and understand how to conduct yourself. You have to know how God wants you to think, say or do anything from morning to evening. The ultimate knowledge and wisdom is found in the Word of God. The Bible's advice to young people, "To have the knowledge, you first must have reverence for the Lord. Stupid people have no respect for wisdom and refuse to learn. (Prov. 1:7). Wisdom will add years to your life. (Prov. 9:11).

The Bible also shows you the rewards of Wisdom when it says, "Learn what I teach you, my son, and never forget what I tell you to do. Listen to what is wise and try to understand it. Yes, beg for knowledge; plead for insight. Look for it as hard as you would for silver or some hidden treasure. If you do, you will know what it means to fear the LORD and you will succeed in learning about God." Prov. 2:1-5.

I have quoted the bible but I know all Holly Books have the similar message to young people like you. It does not matter what faith you are; Christian, Moslem, Hindu, Jew and so on, what matters is that if you have fear of God, and lead your life according to His word, you will have a prosperous life.

But how is the fear of God seen in you? It is through your daily conduct. Start with a Prayer. Thank God for giving you another opportunity to live. Ask God to guide you through the day and protect you from all evil. Show love to all, respect everyone and be kind to strangers. Always act with honesty and be humble in success. When in difficulties, seek wisdom from God, and never allow your tongue to pronounce immoral words. Take time to learn more about your faith and practice it as required. Do not wait for your parents to push you. Actively pursue knowledge of God, because He is the base of your future success and source of true happiness.

May the LORD guide you through your youth!

You have to know how God wants you to think, say or do anything from morning to evening. The ultimate knowledge and wisdom is found in the Word of God.

3

Dream Big

Nelson Mandela once said, "There is no passion to be found playing small – in settling for a life that is less than the one you are capable of living."

At your age, there must be many thoughts that run through your mind and most probably the main one being who exactly you would like to be when you grow up; what kind of life you will lead and what career you will pursue. Whatever it is that you are trying to figure out, make sure that is it BIG!

How will you know that what you are settling for is big? How does it sound to you? If it is not scaring you, know it is not big enough. Does it sound attainable? If the answer is yes, then go back and dream again. Tell it to your friends and watch their response. If they call you insane, mad and crazy then know that it is Big enough, so start working on it.

Just imagine the Wright Brothers, Orville, and Wilbur, who invented the airplane. What do you think people thought of them, insane? That time cars were already there, so thinking of a car that could fly, must have sounded crazy. But they had a dream that no other person had ever thought of and they went on to accomplish it. It was never easy but they persevered, now look at how the whole world is enjoying the fruits of their dream.

Look at our very own brother from Tandale, Diamond Platnumz, the music star, who came from humble beginnings but never allowed his situation to stop him from pursuing his big dream. He found many guys in the music industry who were locally successful but with small dreams, he worked with them and then beat them and now is the star of Africa and the World. His songs are resonating in the waves of Tandale, Johannesburg, Lagos, London and New York. That is the magic of dreaming Big!

Look at Mbwana Samatta, our football star from Mbagala market. With Big dreams, he came and conquered Simba, won the African Club Football Championship with TP Mazembe in Congo DRC, became Africa's Best player in year 2015 and now is one of the stars of the European Champions League with his team Genk. That is what a Big dream looks like.

Dream Big

Let me give you one more example to make sure that you understand me well. Julius Kambarage Nyerere, the Father of the Nation Tanzania, and the greatest African leader, in 1950s lead the Tanganyika independence movements while in his 30s. Against all odds, he successfully achieved his goal and secured peaceful independence for Tanganyika in 1961, at the age of 39 years.

There are many examples that I could give you here, but my message to you is simple and clear. Dream Big, and then persistently follow up. I am not saying it will be easy, but I say in the end it will be worthwhile.

Let me leave you with a quote from Christopher Reeve who said, "So many of our dreams at first seem impossible, then they seem improbable, and then, when you summon the will, they soon become inevitable."

"There is no passion to be found playing small – in settling for a life that is less than the one you are capable of living." – Nelson Mandela -

---

4

Parents' Pride

Pay attention to what your father and mother tell you, my son. Their teaching will improve your character as a handsome turban or a necklace improves your appearance (Prov. 1:8-9).

Obeying your parents becomes a challenge when you are a teenager. This is the time that you want to spread your wings and do things on your own. You want your independence, and you want to prove that you can be a responsible adult. There is still, at this age or period, a high level of need for parent's guidance because there is still so much you can learn from them.

Your need to understand that parents are there to help and assist you to enter into your own life safe and sound. Their role is not to prevent you from living your personal life, not at all. However, what you have to understand is that parents have been in this world longer and have had experiences and are using the knowledge they have gathered to guide you walk through a safe path towards your dream life.

However, since you are also learning from other people in schools and colleges, you learn from peers, seniors, teachers, mentors, books and other media. It is very likely that your life's perspective might differ from that of your parents in some areas. When situations like these happen, you as a child have to remember the following principals;

Always listen to your parents. And think twice before you respond.

Show respect to your parents when they speak to you even when you feel that you do not agree with their position. What you should remember is that your parents are also human beings and that they might not be right all the time. So when you differ with them seek to understand, ask questions and calmly communicate your opinion. They will understand you and they will appreciate your approach and maturity.

The best way to show obedience to your parents is to communicate with them as openly as possible. For example, talk to them about your school life. Talk to them about your challenges and your dreams. Try to be as close and as open to your parents as possible. It is the best way they will understand what you are going through and figure out how best to support you.

Obedience to your parents will reduce frictions and allow you to grow in a peaceful environment.

Remember parents sacrifice a lot for your well being. They work the whole day for your prosperity. They lose their sleep for your safety. They spend countless hours praying for you. There will be nothing you will ever do that will repay this.

The only way you can reward your parents is being obedient to them.

When you do that they will be happy. They will bless you. Their blessings will open doors of success in your life. Your father will be proud of you, and your mother's heart will be filled with joy.

However, obedience should not end with parents alone, but all people, especially elders and the authority. Hillary Clinton wrote a book titled, It Takes a Village. Yes, indeed. It takes many people to bring up a child to maturity. More so in the African life setting where extended families are still strong.

Obedience will save you from many troubles of youth.

Parents' Pride

It will be the base of your wise adult life, which will further your growth into a responsible citizen, loving parent, and a caring spouse.

Therefore, make a determination to become a person your parents will be proud of.

Try to be as close and open to your parents as possible, it is the best way they will understand what you are going through and figure out how best to support you.

5

Finish your Greens

You must have heard this common adage that says, "You are what you eat." I wish it was otherwise, but that is the truth. At a young age, our parents keep insisting on eating the food they give us even when it is not our favorite. Have you ever asked yourself why your mother insists that you finish your greens?

When I was in primary school and in my early years of secondary school I used to be the fattest guy in my class. I was so heavy that my, then Rector, now Bishop Rwoma, decided to enroll me in the school football team's jogging program although I was a basketball player. My weight caused concern to many. However, the jogging program could not help much.

After high school, I changed my eating habits. I started working part-time, so I could no longer eat as I used to, and after a few months, I lost a lot of weight. I felt so good. Then I realized that the body weight is a reflection of what one eats. No wonder my mother insisted on the greens.

You might be experiencing the same eating challenges as I used to. My mother insisted on the greens because I liked meat the more. These days it is even more challenging. There is much more junk food than at my time. When you walk into KFC, McDonalds, Steers and the like, what you get is processed and long preserved meat. Oh! The taste is mouth watering, but not very healthy.

Eating right is a habit like any other. You have to develop it. The earlier you start the better. Good news is that it is not costly. You can start today.

Very often I meet people who want to reduce their weight. They have a great goal but running a wrong strategy. Most people think their body weight can be reduced by going to a gym or doing other physical exercises. I don't think so. The strategy that works for me and that I wish to share is that body weight can only be increased or reduced by the content and amount of food you take. This is what I did and have been doing and that is why I succeeded to maintain my weight ever since. Physical exercise is mainly for increasing body strength and plays a small role in body weight regulation.

This reminds me about Ahmed, my former colleague, who was almost lost his life because of being too much overweight. One day he collapsed and while in hospital he was told to reduce his weight from 120kg to 80kg. Gym trainers advised him to check his food intake for some weeks before he could start exercising.

So as a young person, I advise you to keep your body weight in check all the time. Have a plan. Don't take anything that comes. Take your time to study about proper nutrition according to your lifestyle. If you are not getting good results, you may have to meet a nutritionist.

The most important take away from this chapter is that, if you want to maintain the right body weight then you have to eat right as well. Regulate the portion of food of every meal. Eat just enough and stop. You do not have to finish a full plate. But if your plate is full of greens, just finish them!

Eating right is a habit like any other. You have to develop it. The earlier you start the better. Good news is that, it is not costly. You can start today.

6

Home Alone

Oh, I used to enjoy the movie by John Hughes, titled Home Alone. What a wonderful comedy film. It is a 1990s film but if you have not watched it yet, please make a point to watch it soon. I am sure you will enjoy this movie which became the highest grossing live-action comedy film of all time.

In this movie, a boy, Kevin Mcallister, is mistakenly left behind when his family flies to Paris for their Christmas vacation. Kevin isn't worried about being home alone and is brave enough to fight two burglars.

Apart from making me laugh, I draw a big lesson from Kevin. I want you to learn it too.

Now, ask yourself, if today you were left alone at home, how would you fare? Would you cook, clean the house, clean the bathrooms, arrange the living room, make your bed, do the dishes, wash your clothes and press your clothes? Would you know where the salt is, or sugar, or plates or glasses? Can you find your way to the market? Do you have any idea of the price of a kilo of tomatoes, rice, sembe, onions, coconut or matango? My friend, how long would you survive alone at home?

Now, I am concerned with this because a day is coming when you will be forced by circumstances to leave home and start your life alone. It might not be soon, but it is coming. So, get prepared.

All those I have mentioned above are just some of the house chores that are daily handled by someone at home. Now, that someone has to be you too. You have to live at home like a team member, not a spectator. Participate in daily house chores.

House chores are for girls and boys. House chores make you valuable and dependable in your family. You stop being a parasite that is there to suck all the money and food while adding no value to your family.

The good thing about house chores is that they prepare you for your future. They give you hands on life experience. It does not matter whether you are a boy or girl, learn how to cook, do the dishes, clean the house, make your bed, wash your clothes and look after your young brothers and sisters. When you can confidently perform any duties at home, that means you will be

Home Alone

much more confident when you will start living by yourself.

Saturday, May 5th, 2001 is one of the days I cannot forget in my life. This is the day I left home to start my life. To start a life I had dreamt for many years. Living by myself. Living alone. It was an experience like no other. For a long time, I had thought of the idea of being able to take care of myself and become my own leader. Everyone around me thought I was insane. I had left behind a very comfortable lifestyle, where almost everything was available and in plenty. I mean a nice house, beautiful furniture, good neighborhood, cars, house-helpers and off course loving family members. Despite all that, I left and went to start my life in a very humble place deep in Sinza.

I was like Kevin, confident and ready to face life by myself. I had graduated from years of home training. I was ready to lead my life my own way.

I am sharing this with you so that you also understand the importance of house chores.

From today, do not wait to be asked, told or forced to perform a house duty, demand duties. Change your attitude. It should be you now to demand to be involved even when your mother tells you not to do dishes because the house-maid is there.

Demand to participate in house cleaning, washing your own clothes and those of others if available. Switch off the Television and throw away your smartphone until all the house chores are done. Seek personal satisfaction in how you have been involved in the house works during the day. Count the hours and duties you have performed in the day before going to bed and plan to do same or better the next day.

Because I can assure you, house chores are your free hands-on life lessons that will be most important when you will have no other person to turn to in the future. You are being trained. Enjoy them and master them as well.

If you learn and act on this advice, I can assure you that you will enter your future with full confidence, happy and responsible.

House chores make you valuable and dependable in your family. You stop being a parasite that is there to suck all the money and food while adding no value to your family.

7

Smart & Clean

I once read that, you have only one chance to make the first impression.
Recently I attended the parents meeting at Liebermann Secondary School where my son, Ishengoma is in form three. It was also a day of celebration where best students in various categories were being awarded. While they awarded best performers in academics, the award to the smartest student caught my attention. I was impressed and wished other students would understand the importance of being well groomed and properly dressed for the occasion.

It is a fact of life that other people will judge you according to your appearance. Studies have shown that people will always remember you according to the first image they stored in their minds, even if you change later.

That means, if a person sees you shabby on your first meeting, that is the image he will store in his brain even if you meet him again while you are smart. Although in the long run, that impression might change, it will take a lot of constant effort to prove otherwise.

At a young age, it is important to know these facts and start to work on them immediately. You have to be mindful of how you appear in public differently. You have to know that you have a duty to create a good impression of yourself in the minds of others, and that can happen if you always look smart.

I am talking about taking care of your body, grooming yourself, choice of clothes, shoes and other accessories.

I am sure you want to be a great person when you grow up. If I ask you to search for a photo of a truly successful person who appears shabby, you might not get it. Why? It is because success is associated with smartness. Look at all successful business people like; Reginald Mengi, Mohamed Dewji, Aliko Dangote; politicians like Barack Obama, John P. Magufuli, Donald Trump; musicians like Michael Jackson, Diamond Platnumz, Beyonce Knowles. They are always well dressed. Always well groomed, smart and clean.

If you have completed college and you are about to

start looking for employment, this topic could not have been more relevant to you. In all job interviews, your appearance matters as much as your CV. The psychology behind it is simple. If you cannot take good care of yourself, how will you be able to take care of a complex company's business?

How you appear shouts louder about you than how your mouth can ever do.

Take good care of yourself, and people will trust you with their matters.

Looking good is a habit. Develop it from now. It is not difficult and it does not require any financial investment. Just change of attitude.

Be clean, be smart! Look good.

It is a fact of life that other people will judge you according to your appearance

8

Eagles flock with Eagles

There is an old English adage that says, "Tell me your friends and I will tell you who you are." This old statement is still true up to this day. As a young person, you have to understand from this early age that your habits are always influenced by the habits of the people you are close with. Whether you are in secondary school, college or have just completed college you have to look at your friends and see if you have common habits and hobbies. Because they say, birds of the same feather flock together. It will be very strange to see people of totally different habits hanging out together. Friends are always attracted to people who look like themselves.

I love football and some of my friends are football lovers. When I meet these friends more than 80% of our conversation is about football. While my three favorite

Eagles flock with Eagles

teams are Real Madrid, Chelsea, and Yanga, my close friends love Manchester United, Liverpool and Simba. Like all fans, we tease each other and look forward to the results of our next games. It is always fun.

Now with social media, I am in various groups with people of diverse interests from faith groups, Bankers, Rotarians, Colleagues, to Schoolmates and classmates. I know for sure the more I stay close to these people the more they will influence my thinking and habits.

When I was young my mother used to tell me not to play with some friends while she did not have problems with others. As a child, I did not know why. I remember how whenever I would ask for a permission to go play at my friend's place, my mother would always remind me not to go to some homes. Now that I am also a parent, I understand why my mother never liked some of the friends. She wanted to protect me from habits that she had noted in those friends. She knew the principal very well that if I play with these guys, their habits will become mine too.

If you want to become a good student and later grow up to become a great person in life you have to start now. You have to choose the type of people you would like to influence your habits. If any of your friends have some bad habits, tell them to change, otherwise reduce the time you spend with them. Look around to see if there are people who you admire for their good conduct and forge a friendship with them.

Avoid people who are not honest, who are indiscipline, people who steal other people's items, liars, dirty, lazy and not God fearing. While these habits may appear small or insignificant, they tend to become big as their holders grow. Friends like these will pull you down and drag you into their bad habits. Avoid them.

The good news is that you have all the power to choose who gets close to you and who should not. I ask you to assess all your friends and from now take action!

Birds of the same feather flock together. Eagles flock with eagles, not crows.

You have to choose the type of people you would like to influence your habits. If any of your friends have some bad habits, tell them to change otherwise reduce the time you spend with them.

9

Read, Read & Read!

Ask me about what my greatest hobby now is, I will answer without hesitation, reading. If you ask me when did I develop this hobby, I will say as early as when I knew how to read. This is when I was about seven years old because this is the time I joined primary school. I enjoyed the stories in our textbooks. Later, reading became a tool that equipped my ever-inquisitive mind.

When I was in standard three, while reading a Chinese magazine, I saw a subscription form. With a lot of enthusiasm, I quickly filled it and gave it to my mother to post it for me. A few weeks of waiting passed and the enthusiasm died off. It is now more than thirty years, but I can still remember how happy I felt on the day my mother returned home with a big envelope with my name on it. It was a parcel from China. It was a pictorial magazine, with a few postcards and a triangular flag. Those became my most valuable treasures for a long time.

Since then I have read hundreds of articles in magazines and books. I love books and I buy books and magazines whenever I get an opportunity to do so.

Reading has made me become unique from the rest of my peers. As a professional Accountant and Banker, I have come to realize that my life's perspective was quite different from many of my colleagues. I would confidently say that my quick rise up the corporate ladder could be attributed to my broad understanding of the world which has always made me confident in my interactions with my seniors, peers, and juniors.

When I reflect back, I fail to find any other reason for my employment as the Financial Controller of Habib African Bank when I was just 25 years old. At this time I was already a Certified Public Accountant without a prior experience in the banking sector. I believe it was my mental attitude and my capability to communicate confidently that captivated the CEO, Mr. Manzar Kazmi, to recruit me for such an important role at that young age. I can confidently say I was the youngest bank financial controller in the country.

The good news is that reading habit can be developed by anyone who wishes to do so. If you are still in secondary school, college or just started your career you can slowly develop this noble habit.

Read Read & Read!

Reading is the habit of the great. If you want to become great in life you have no choice but to make reading one of your hobbies. The reading I am talking about here is the extra reading other than your textbooks or professional mandatory references.

What you should know is that reading does to your mind what physical exercise does to your body muscles. That means as you see people exercising trying to keep their body muscles strong, going to the gym or running along the road that is the same thing that happens to your mind when you read. Reading broadens your understanding of the world, cultures, and people. If you wish to be successful like Bill Gates, Warren Buffet, Mark Zuckerberg, Aliko Dangote, Julius Nyerere or Nelson Mandela you have to develop the habit of reading. All these great minds are known to be voracious readers. You have to be equally hungry for knowledge.

You will note that I have not said which kind of books you should be reading. I want you to develop the habit of reading all kind of books. If you are still in school read textbooks, and then read self-development books, books about history, psychology, novels, politics, biographies, and poetry. Simply read any book or magazine that you can lay your hands on!

— *Ntangeki Nshala* —

Reading is the habit of the great. If you want to become great in life you have no choice but to make reading one of your hobbies.

10

Sit in Front

When I was in primary school I preferred to seat at the back of the class, the back bencher. While many colleagues took seats at the back for different reasons; some because they are tall, some because they could not find the space in front, but my reason was unique. I sat behind because I wanted to hide from teachers. Don't get me wrong, I was never a trouble maker, actually, I used to be one of the gentle and quietest. I never knew the real cause then, but now I know, it was because of I lacked self-confidence. It is ironic because I was still among those who always did well in class.
After many years of observation, I came to a conclusion that most those who seat behind are those who lack self-confidence. You may also do short research. I have observed this in schools, colleges and in workplaces. When a group of people is called by their elder be it

teachers, or boss you will see that the most confident will be in front and those less confident will move slowly so that they stand behind.

Lack of self-confidence may not be directly related to performance in short-term, but in the long run, it will affect your capacity to take on challenges and move forward.

Not being confident means not believing in your capabilities to handle certain tasks. The key word here is belief. Belief is mostly not the reality.

Recently I saw a video clip of two Masai morani hunting in the Serengeti. From far they saw a pride of six lions attacking a buffalo. Unbelievably, the morani walked straight to the lions, and all six lions run away leaving the meat behind. The morani cut a sizable piece and walked away. Now, that is confidence at its best. Scaring six lions with a stick and a knife is incredible.

This is exactly what happens to you when you develop self-confidence. It enables you to stand up to mighty challenges and solve them. Many a times fear is just a result of pessimistic imaginations. You think of defeat or failure before even trying.

Sit in front

The good news is that confidence can be learned, practiced and mastered. The best way to become confident is to be confident about what you know, what you can. Always be prepared and well knowledgeable about subjects or things you are expected to know. That means don't be lazy.

The other effective way of building and gaining self-confidence is replacing your fear of failure with your desire for success. See, when your desire for success is big enough, all your energy and attention is focused there so much so that you cannot see any obstacles and if there are any, your energy will simply overcome them.

So if you are in school or college, believe in your capability to achieve whatever you are set to achieve. Confidently stand for your desired destination and you will see success follow you.

Since practice makes perfect, from now onwards take the seat in front. It works because this is what I applied when I wanted to gain confidence in myself. Whenever you are called in a group, just be in front. You will realize two important things; first, you will get a clear message from the speaker and second if there are any opportunities to be grabbed, you will be the closest. The bonus point is that, when you are in front, the view is always great!

Therefore, sit in front no matter what.

Lack of self-confidence may not be directly related to performance in short-term, but in the long run, it will affect your capacity to take on challenges and move forward.

11

Volunteer to Lead

The best way to learn is by practicing. Practice makes perfect. This is how I want you to learn leadership.

When you lead yourself you also learn to lead others. Leadership comes from within and not without. The way you will lead others is the manifestation of who you are inside. It shows who you really are, the real you. That will be the base of your leadership.

In secondary schools, we have the Head Boy or Head Girl and the cabinet of prefects. In college we have presidents of students and their respective ministers. Sometimes their election is as hot as the national elections. Some students are very passionate about leadership to an extent that they carry out fully fledged campaigns.

Once they become leaders in these colleges, they normally go on to become leaders in many places they go to after college. Why? Because of they have the vision of what they want to accomplish in their lifetime.

For most of us, we lead a school or college life quietly without any funfair. We do not want to get involved in community or public activities. We do not want to be held responsible for matters of our communities. We want to save our energy, I do not know for what use. If you are this type of a person, I have news for you. Stop it! Stop living a passive life. Don't be lazy. Don't be selfish. Go out and get your hands dirty. Get involved.

There are many benefits of being involved in leading others. I understand you may not want to become the Head Girl, or Head Boy or the President of the students association. That's fine. But you can be a class monitor, sports captain, a debate group leader, or a book reading group leader, you can volunteer to lead an assignment issued by your teacher. You do not have to have a title. You just need to stand for the best interest of your fellows.

The best way to learn how to lead people is by leading. And if you want to become a great leader in future you have to start now, with small groups and small responsibilities. If you cannot be elected, volunteer.

When you become the leader of a group, like a class, school, college or any kind of a team you become the custodian of their vision. You become the guardian of their values and you become the center of the manifestation of the dream. You become responsible for steps forward or backward. All eyes are on you.

John Maxwell said, 'leadership is influence." I agree with him. As soon as you become the group leader, members will start listening to your directions and they make themselves available for the sake of the vision. Soon you will realize that people will support you because your success is their success.

In the process of leading others, you also learn how to communicate effectively, how to manage your time, you appreciate the importance of punctuality, you learn how to listen and debate. Through leading others you learn that being a leader does not mean being the best and that makes you humble. You learn how to control your emotions, and appreciate the importance of self-discipline. All these can be best learned by practicing leadership. The best thing about taking leadership roles early in your life is that you will make mistakes and learn from them when stakes are low and the cost is minimal.

Through leading others you learn that being a leader does not mean being the best and that makes you humble.

12

Family First

We live in very interesting times. Times when people from different countries, continents, races, gender, faiths, and ideologies are connected through the social media. Social media has become such a powerful tool that people don't talk to each other but rather keep busy on their phones chatting. Physical interactions have been replaced by virtual interactions.

Social media has taken all of us by storm because of our human nature. We are social creatures. We want to belong to communities and groups. We want to be among others and when we speak we want the attention. Fortunately, social media is giving us all that and in a very simple manner. By a click of a button, thousands get our message, and through our small but smart gadgets, we receive enormous amount of information as it happens.

Family First

However, all these tools have not been able to quench the real human need. Although social media is useful, your social media tribe cannot give you as much love, compassion and care as what your family can give.

I recently saw an observation on social media when one person was calling for attention and cautioning people not to rely too much on social media virtual friends and forget the real people close to us. He expressed his disappointment. He said that he recently fell ill and had to be hospitalized for around three weeks. That as a social media fun with thousands of followers, he quickly informed his friends about his situation to which he also sent a photo taken while on a hospital bed with drips hanging around him. Three weeks in hospital, the only people that came were his family members and handful friends, mostly coworkers. Not a single social media friend took time to visit him and yet he has thousands of them on Twitter, Facebook, WhatsApp, LinkedIn, and Instagram.

What a great lesson there! While social media friends can be helpful, there is a limit to what they can really offer to your life. Social media friends can never be as useful as the real friends that you make in real life. The first real friends are your family, your parents, brothers, and sisters. These are your first inner cycle. In Africa, the inner cycle may include some of uncles, aunties, and cousins. These are the people that you have to be close to as much as possible. Sometimes relations with some may not be the best, but remember when things are really bad; they will turn up to help.

It is your family that will sacrifice their pleasures; time, career and anything else for you. They will take leave to help you when you are sick, they will fight for your wellbeing and success. Workmates will be there but they will never sacrifice their career for you, but family members can put their career on hold if need be. Very rarely you might be lucky to have a friend who will go extra miles for you, who will risk it all for you.

I understand that at a young age, one might not completely understand the importance of family, because you are now busy with friends, who seem to be very good to you. They might be good, but often only good in good times.

Therefore at this young age, you should know, understand and appreciate the importance of family in your life, and cherish it. These are the people to trust the most than anyone else. Share with them your dreams and plans so that they give you support and honesty feedback. Visit them and call them as often as possible. Physically visit

— *Family First* —

them and get time to talk to them. Share with them your ambitions, successes, and challenges. These are the people who will cry when you cry and laugh when you laugh because they feel how you feel. They will give a shoulder for you to cry on when you are down and will stand with you without judging you. In the end, these are the people who know who you truly are!

Although social media is useful, your social media tribe cannot give you as much love, compassion and care as what your family can give.

13

Fear Fear!

If you want to be remembered as old and wise you must first be young and stupid. There is no better time to take risks and try things than at a young age. Because if things go well you will be praised and considered genius and if you fail the family and community will be ready to accommodate you. Especially when the event was done in good faith.

This reminds me of one day in my village primary school. What seemed to be a simple act of trial defined my future. On this very normal day, a Catholic priest worked in our class accompanied by our Head teacher. After a few greetings, the priest asked whether there were any students interested in joining seminary school. A few friends of mine put up their hands but I didn't. A curious Head teacher approached me looking straight in my eyes asked me why was I not interested. He knew me very well, so he expected me to be the best fit, but I

— *Fear Fear!* —

said no, without any good reason. He knew it was sheer lack of courage and confidence. I was afraid. I was filled with the fear of the unknown. The Head teacher asked the priest to give us a week to think about it and contact him.

After that encounter with the Head teacher and the Priest, I took time to think about the opportunity. I critically looked at my life at that school, how we lacked many facilities, no power, no water, very poor classrooms, no good teachers and only one or two people would pass the standard seven national exams. Then I built an imaginary picture. If I gave a try to the idea of joining a seminary and passed. I imagined on how beautiful our seminary would be, the boarding school life which would be much better than a village life I was living in. What if I became a priest and how great I would be among people? After comparing my present and my imaginary future, I had a good reason to accept the idea and took a leap of faith, took the exams and passed out of hundreds and the rest is history!!

When I look back at this I can't thank my Head teacher enough. He had confidence in me. What if I had allowed my fear of failure overpower my desire for success? Would I have ever got the opportunity to study at one of the best schools of our time? A school with best teachers, facilities and among all, best students. How would my life be today? Where would I have been today, writing this book or somewhere in the village broke and broken?

We are all born with special uniqueness and sometimes our uniqueness may not be appreciated by our families. You may have talents that may not lead you to the conventional life that your parents want for you. If you genuinely feel that your talent is your destiny, do not be afraid to express yourself clearly and consistently until you are understood. Sadly, I have come to understand that many people end up living life much below their potential, just because they did not work on the unique talents. This is either because they were afraid of failure, or because their families did not allow them to.

I have also come to realize that failure accounts for very little to people's shattered dreams, but the biggest killer of people's dreams is simply fear of failure. Just FEAR! Not attempting at all.

So I urge you to be courageous. Stand for what you feel is good. Try. Know that all great discoveries are a result of many previous failed trials. You will be amazed by how much help and encouragement you will receive when you follow your dream. When you horn your talent!

Fear Fear!

Your greatest enemy in your life might be fear, as Franklin Roosevelt, the former president of USA, said, "The only thing to fear is fear itself."

I have also come to realize that failure accounts for very little to people's shattered dreams, but the biggest killer of people's dreams is simply fear of failure.

14

Time is Precious

Time management has never been easy even for grown up people more so for the youth. However, we are always told that the most precious asset we all have is time. But it never ceases to amaze me how people handle it carelessly and allow it to wastefully pass.

Have you ever asked yourself why some people manage to accomplish so much in a day while some don't? While some people complete a lot of transactions in 24 hours some fumble around with one or two. There is no magic to this. The answer is simple, time management.

Time management is simply planning your activities for the day and allocating time for each. With this, not even a second is left unplanned for. Every second is allocated and used as intended.

I came to appreciate the importance of time management

Time is Precious

when I was in Secondary school, at St. Mary's Seminary-Rubya. The daily routine at this school included a lot of activities; morning prayers and Holly Mass, silence hours, classes, afternoon Angelus, manual works, sports, evening prayers, all meals and evening 'preps'. At this school, there were no unallocated times. Every single minute was allocated for and it was mandatory to be where you are expected to be, on time. This is a place where being late for a few seconds can land you into serious trouble and be at a wrong place, in a wrong time, is enough to get you packing. This is why many missionary schools always out-perform other schools, not because they have super intelligent students and teachers, but because they optimize the usage of their time.

Therefore, when you are in such a school, you are lucky and so take full advantage of the system and give your best. But for those in colleges or day schools where life is free, you have to take it upon yourself to make sure that you use your time well. If your parents are not there to remind you, well, I am here to do that.

If you want to learn how to do this, you will have to start by analyzing how your typical day runs against the main reason you are here. If you are in college, then you are there to learn. In that case, your activities should be those that complement your learning. In that regard any activity that does not help you learn better, has to be dropped. Do not be afraid to even drop friends who seem to be a distraction to you, or those who pull you into unwanted activities that add no value to your learning. Better be safe than sorry.

Arrange your activities according to their importance in assisting you to learn. Then allocate time for each, without leaving any unallocated minute. In a day there must be resting periods, these have to be allocated too. From the time you get out of bed to the time you go to bed, every minute has to be allocated.

While doing this exercise you will get an opportunity to think and evaluate every move of your day. You will be amazed at the number of activities you can perform in a day. You will discover how much time you always waste on nonsense activities.

Once you have allocated your time, then it is time to implement. Here you will require discipline. Many people can dream, plan and attempt, but it is discipline that will help you follow your plan to the very end.

Time management is simply planning your activities for the day and allocating time for each.

15

Stand the Peer Pressure

Peer pressure is a situation where you are being constantly requested by your friends to behave in a certain way or do certain actions just because they like to do it that way and so should you. In most cases, peer pressure is applied to behaviors that are not positive or actions that are against rules and regulations. If you are not careful you find yourself in trouble.

I remember when I was in secondary school, in form two; a few friends of mine were expelled from school for absconding. What actually happened is that these students had created a habit of going out of school either for drinking or for affairs with girls in the neighborhoods. It was a group of friends, and a few influenced the rest into this bad behavior.

Friends always play a big role to who you become in future. One philosopher once said you are an average of the five people you mostly engage with. In that regard, you have to be very careful of who you make friendship with. In school, students come with different habits from their home, some of which are not positive, be careful. Peer pressure can be very dangerous and costly. It can cost your life.

Many of my friends who were expelled from school never made it past form four. It is very sad because these were very smart young boys who had great potential for a successful life. I am sure they must be regretting their acts. They were definitely childish acts, with catastrophic effects on their lives. Boys who would have been lawyers, doctors, engineers, like many of their classmates, have ended up being peasants and small time traders. Peer pressure shuttered their dreams.

It is worse these days where unethical activities have multiplied. In schools and colleges, there are activities that you have to be very careful with such as drugs, alcohol, early age sexual affairs and the like. Indeed globalization has also come with some negative influences that need to be avoided.

── Stand the Peer Pressure ──

I want you to know that even though your parents cannot see you, or your teachers cannot catch you, bad habits will not spare you. Because just like how my friends' dreams were shattered, yours too could end up the same. Bad habits are addictive. If you will not be caught directly, your health and your poor performance will reveal you, and eventually, all people will know the secret. It might be too late!

I want you to know that even though your parents cannot see you, or your teachers cannot catch you, bad habits will not spare you.

16

Girls Power

Being the father of twins, a boy, and a girl gives me a special opportunity to discuss this matter. When I look at my son, Ishengoma, and my daughter, Nyakato, I see two very different people. At birth, their only difference was their gender, but everything else was the same. However, as they grow up, now as teenagers, their differences couldn't be more obvious. Nature has taken its course. As parents, my wife and I treat them the same and assign them house chores equally. Unfortunately, this is not what is happening in the community at large.

It is headline news when a woman takes over a leadership position in a national or an international organization. It is big news when a woman is elected president of a nation. It is also a big talk of the community when a woman becomes wealthy. And yet the number of women is almost equal to the number of men in the

— Girls Power —

world population. For centuries the situation has been the same, men dominating women, economically, politically, socially and legally.

News flash! The 21st century is turning out to be different. There is a very bright light at the end of the tunnel. The attitude is changing fast, and the girl power is rising. It gives me a special joy inside, that my daughter will have the equal opportunities as my son. Their success in life will be determined by their character and not their gender.

Given the same opportunities, girls can perform as well as the boys. This applies to almost any task. There is no study that has shown that men are better than women intellectually. In that regard, there is no reason whatsoever, that boys are better than girls or vice versa.

It is time for girls to wake up and take their rightful position in the community. Many countries constitutions now offer equal rights between men and women. So girls, rise up and grab this opportunity, and balance this equation.

Eleanor Roosevelt once said, "No one can make you feel inferior without your consent."

We already have examples of women who have shattered the glass ceiling and risen above the norms. We have women Presidents and Heads of state, like Ellen Johnson Sirleaf of Liberia, Angela Merkel of German, and Theresa May of UK to mention but a few. In Tanzania, two people who have served in highest positions in the UN are all women, Prof. Anna Kajumulo Tibaijuka who served as the Under-Secretary-General and the Executive Director of UN-HABITAT and Dr. Asha-Rose Migiro who became the Deputy Secretary General of the UN. The first President of the Pan-African Parliament was a Tanzanian woman, Dr. Gertrude Mongella.

We have women Nobel Peace Prize winners like Wangari Maathai, Ellen Johnson Sirleaf, and Laymah Gbowee.

Any girl in this 21st century has no reason to despair because many women, from all walks of life, have proven beyond reasonable doubt that they can perform as well as men. Be it in Business, Politics, Civil Service, and Religion.

My grandfather, who I consider to have been born ahead of his time, took all his 9 girls to school. He stood against community pressure because sending girls to school was considered a waste of money. His vision and courage changed the fortunes of the family, the community and the world at large.

Girls Power

While I am an advocate for Girl power, I am in no way encouraging girls to abandon their duties as girls. All traditions have their ways of distribution of duties in their families and communities. However, these duties have to be fair, legal and nondiscriminatory.

When Hillary Clinton was delivering her 2016 concession speech she said, "To all the little girls who are watching, never doubt that you are valuable and powerful and deserving of every chance and opportunity in the world to pursue and achieve your own dreams."

I say 21st century is the Girls' Power century, stand up, dream big and allow nothing to stop you from accomplishing your dreams.

It gives me a special joy inside, that my daughter will have equal opportunities as my son.

17

Boys to Men

As a young boy, I witnessed a few rough encounters between my parents. While I love my father so much, I noted that he had habit of mistreating my mother especially when he was drunk. At times small issues would be turned into a full blown scuffle. I used to be scared. I felt sorry for my mother for I knew she deserved a better treatment.
A few years later, I had an opportunity to live with my aunt. There I experienced a very different life, a life where a husband and wife would always be happy with each other. Talk calmly and discuss matters and expressing their different opinion on issues in a very peaceful, friendly and respectful way. That is the time I made a decision that when I become a man, mature, with family, that is a way of life that I will emulate.

I am now married for more that fourteen years and I am yet to find any reason to raise my hand against my wife.

Boys to Men

I love her and we have built a wonderful family together. We have been through ups and downs together, we are not perfect, many times we have not agreed on issues, but we all understand that we all are human beings and not angels. Sometimes we err but we help each other to change for better. Above all, I respect her as a mature human being.

I can understand the generation to which my father belonged; many men behaved the way he behaved. A generation where power belonged to men and the way to show it was through habits like those my father exhibited. Many friends of mine have given me almost similar scenarios in their families. At one point I thought it was a generational issue so it would end with that generation. But I was dead wrong!

Our media continues to report many horrible cases of domestic violence. It pains me more, at this age, especially when even some of the people that I know still mistreat their wives. These are people who are successful; well educated, well traveled, doing well financially but for some reasons, they have failed to grow up to become real men, gentlemen.

If you are a boy reading this, I want you to take a vow to become a man, a gentleman. Gentlemen are confident in themselves and respectful to all. Gentlemen respect and protect women against anybody or anything, physically and emotionally and under no circumstances would they harass any woman. Gentlemen work hard to give their families good life. Gentlemen love their children and teach them to become better people through their own lives. Gentlemen live happy lives because they receive a lot of love from people around them. People like to be around gentlemen.

No matter what: you never hit a woman. There's no excuse. There's no possible argument to the contrary. There's no "what if?" and there's no qualifier. Gentlemen don't hit women. Never!

If you want to live a life full of success, you have to decide now to grow up into a man, a real man, a gentleman.

Gentlemen respect and protect women against anybody or anything, physically and emotionally and under no circumstances would they harass any woman.

18

Truth will set you Free

When we were young our parents taught us to speak the truth all the time, and that is the way of life we knew. But as we grow older we realize sometimes truth leads to punishment. Then when we do something wrong and we are asked about it, we want to avoid the punishment by not saying the truth. Unfortunately, we get away with it, and that is the time we know that not saying the truth can be better. At that time we may think that it is just a small thing, so it is ok. I have even heard some mature people say that it's a white lie, no way.

There can never be a white lie. A lie is a lie and is a bad behavior. When you lie you hurt your conscience, and when you keep lying your conscience becomes adamant and senseless and fearless. All evil starts with a single, simple, white lie. When you start lying you do not stop.

As a young person, you should know from very early that you are expected, to be honest, all the time no matter what. Honesty means saying the truth, nothing but the truth, no matter the situation or consequences. You may ask yourself if honesty is this important, why is that many people are not. Warren Buffett, one of the world's richest people once said, "Honesty is a very expensive gift, Don't expect it from cheap people."

If you want to be successful in life, and you want to be a respected person, I encourage you to be 100% honest and speak the truth from now, and from today! You will realize it is very simple to build this habit although it may not be easy.

If you are in school or college you may seem to get away with so many problems by lying, and so it is common to lie. But if from now you refuse to lie, your close friends will be the first to attack you as if you have lost your mind. I am sure you will experience huge resistance from peers who are used to an ordinary you, while they do not know that you have decided to stand out and become extraordinary. I can assure you that the moment you decide to become 100% honest and speak the truth,

Truth will set you Free

you will automatically start being careful in what you do and how you do it because you do not want to find yourself in a situation that may force you to compromise your principal. And if you persevere, it will become your normal habit, and that will be the beginning of your journey to greatness. You will slowly join great leaders like Julius Nyerere and Nelson Mandela, who were so strong that they never compromised their principals because of convenience. Julius Nyerere lead Tanzania for many years but never stole wealth for himself like many African leaders of his time. After his presidency he lead a simple life like any common citizen. Nelson Mandela lead the fight against social, economic and political oppression in South Africa, and he was jailed for 27 years but never left his fight until apartheid was defeated and became the first president of free South Africa.

As I stated earlier, being honest is simple but not easy. It is hard and costly. It will cost your friends, your freedom and sometimes your life pleasures. But in the end, it is worth all of that, because it is invaluable.

All evil starts with a single, simple, white lie.

19

Devil's Workshop

"An idle mind is the workshop of the devil."

Again this reminds me of the early boarding school days. One evening our teacher walked in the class only to find us busy making noise. He cautioned us while repeating this phrase several times, "An idle mind is the workshop of the devil."

Indeed when your mind stays idle, the devil will put it into use. That is when crazy ideas come to you and find yourself in funny situations. Sometimes I think the energy that we have when we are young pushes us into action. So when there are no productive engagements to be taken care of, the energy will be directed into unproductive activities.

When I completed my secondary level school in 1993, I had to spend about eight months at home waiting for results and selection to high school. At first, I wondered how I would spend all this time at home, almost alone because at this time all my brothers and sisters were either in school or in college. My father would work on the farm all day and my mother who was a civil servant, a nurse, would go to work, from early morning to late evening. I was literally home alone. That meant doing all the house chores, cooking, taking care of the cows and selling milk to our fellow villagers.

This was one of the most challenging times of my life. My day used to start at 6 am in the morning and end when I crash on my bed at around 9 pm. My day used to be packed with work such that I would not notice how a day would pass. I literally had to juggle my duties to run them smoothly. Eight months passed unbelievably fast, and I found myself having to leave for high school.

This period taught me one great lesson, that as a young person, you have within you unfathomable amount of energy that is waiting to be put into use. I also realized that laziness is a state of mind and not a state of your body. If you tune your mind to the right frequency your can perform wonders no matter the size of your body. But if you let your mind lie idle, the strength of your body will count for nothing.

During the same period of eight months my close friend, John, went to spent time away from home, in the city of Dar es Salaam. He had some good time there but I later came to know that he had a lot of free time. His guardians were business people and had little time to look after their children. John became idle, and as you already know, an idle mind is the workshop of the devil. During this time he developed bad habits. However the impact of his bad habits could not be noted immediately. The moment of truth came when the High School results were out. John, a smart boy who had scored brilliantly in secondary school performed unbelievably poorly in High school.

When you are on school holidays, you should know that you are given that time to rest from the routine of formal studies, but not from performing other duties. Smart young boys and girls use their holiday time learning and performing other productive activities, be it at home or away from home. Do not allow yourself to spend hours in front of the TV or playing games in your Smartphone. Use this time to learn. Do house chores, read books or learn new skills.

I got my first job as the Financial Controller of Habib African Bank, at age 25, about a week after completing my CPA courses. How was that possible? Simple! For two years prior to completion of my studies I was working part time at my Aunt's company as an accountant. Therefore by the time became a Certified Professional Accountant (CPA), I was ready, confident and qualified.

You can also ask your parents, if possible, to take you with them when they go to work. Go hang around there. Be a person to help arrange files, make photocopies, answer calls. Be there to receive customers, or deliver documents. Volunteer to work for free. If your parents are not in a position to help, ask others, relatives or neighbors. Look for any possibilities to volunteer, because through that you will come across real-world challenges and experiences that you cannot get in school or college.

If you tune your mind to the right frequency your can perform wonders no matter the size of your body, but if you let your mind lie idle, the strength of your body will count for nothing.

20

Work Hard!

In 1988 when I joined Rutabo Preparatory Seminary school, I was around 12 years old. It was one of the happiest times in my life. Joining the school means I managed to beat hundreds of kids from many primary schools spread in four districts of Kagera Region. I remember how my father accompanied me on my first trip and the way we were welcomed at the school. The environment seemed perfect and senior students looked very smart in their brown khaki shorts and short sleeve white shirts. This was one of the best elite schools of our time. The seminary.

As the classes started and tests were given out, I started to realize that this was not a normal group of students that I was familiar with in my old school. This was one of the best groups of talented students, everyone looking to outperform the other. I remember when the results of our first monthly test were out, almost everyone fell in shock. It was unbelievable to most because everyone

— Work Hard —

used to be the king of the class at their old schools. This was the moment of truth for many. This was a different league and a different playing ground. Tough exams, tough competition.

Next morning, the school rector, Fr. Medard Weyemele walked in, with his hands folded behind. Posed and then rectified his spectacles, gave a cynical smile and said, "What happened?" then he changed his tone to a sharp voice, "Guys you need to pull up your socks, and remember, you came here to study, so stop playing around. If you continue like this, I will kick you out!"

I remember our seniors teasing us, "guys you have to read until your eyes turn red!"

If you are in school or went to school or college, you might have encountered a similar situation. However, after my school and college years, I came to one revelation. Revelation to a secret. This is the secret for truly enjoying the school life and coming out with all your head held high. This is the secret that all professionals you meet have used in their years in school and college. I mean all professional, be it Doctors, engineers, Accountant, Bankers, Architects or Teachers. The secret is, "Study Hard."

I can assure you that you will have no place in this 21st Century if you do not study hard now. Whether you are in the Ordinary level, High school, in college or just completed your degree. The 21st Century has no place for lazy people. It does not matter how well off your parents are currently.

One thing you have to understand is that, while you are in school your studying hard brings you good grades. For me that is important, but is not the real prize. The most precious gift you will earn for studying hard is the habit. The habit of studying hard shapes you into a hard working man in future. This is the real prize. Because if you ultimately want to live a life full of success, you will have to work hard for it.

See, if you become hard working at a young age you will be successful in whatever you do and that means you might start to make millions much early in your life. You will probably become a young millionaire. Isn't that exciting enough?

So while your parents might be telling you to study hard and you ignore them, thinking it is their usual litany, you are wrong. You better listen. If your teachers insist that you finish your homework, if they insist you remain silent during studying hours, obey them. Their advice is invaluable.

Work Hard

Remember schools and colleges are not free; someone is working hard to make you be there. And how are you planning to re-pay them? I can assure you, there is only one way to repay your parents for paying for your education. That is by passing your exams!

So while they work hard to keep you here, you study hard and make them cheer!

The habit of studying hard shapes you into a hard working man in future.

Ntangeki Nshala

21

A Myth of a Private Life

It is now common knowledge that public leaders' lives are scrutinized and are closely followed up by many people in such a way that whatever they do is of public interest. In simple terms, public leaders live public lives. Nothing is private for them. That is well accepted by many people now.

This then means that you and I, who are not public leaders, live a private life.

For many years I have been asking myself whether there is ever a private life. More so in this 21st Century. What does private life really mean? Does that mean whatever I do should not concern others? Or it means no one is looking at what I do?

A Myth of a Private Life

May be you are also asking yourself what does this topic got to do with me at this young age.

See, I am writing this book to help you create a future of your dreams. The best future you could potentially have. Now, the way you live your life now has everything to do with your future. If you consider your life private, then you will live believing whatever you do have nothing to do with your future success. This is wrong.

There is no private life. The concept of private life is just a myth.

Whatever you say, however you say it will concern some people; your parents, friends or leaders. Whatever you do will involve or affect some people, be it your peers, your neighbors, colleagues, or strangers. Your lifestyle will catch the attention of some people like your parents, siblings, aunt, uncle, local leaders, church or friends. So if all these people are going to be interested in your life, or affected by what you do, or alarmed by how you live, so what is private about your life?

Get it right, there is no private life. You are not an island. You live with people, and people are watching you. Parents, brothers, sisters, aunties, uncles, neighbors, teachers, friends, strangers and everyone is watching you. You are on a constant watch, like in a Big Brother

House. Your life is public! Simple and clear.

So what then? It is a big deal, my friend.

See, a few years ago we were about to hire someone for a very senior post in a bank. He had very nice papers and well experienced. He seemed to be a perfect fit for the job. Out of curiosity, we reached out to his former colleagues in his last two organizations. All five gave a negative recommendation. They were his friends, people he worked with, his peers. These are people who knew him well. They knew his character.

You see what I mean now!

It is a fact of life that you will be in constant evaluation by other people. People you least think about. These people know your character perfectly well. They know what you are capable of and what you are not. They know your technical ability and your leadership capacity. They know your hobbies and your favorite drink.

These are the same people who will recommend you to their bosses so that you can also join their organization or will alert their bosses not to make that mistake. These are your classmates, school mates, college mates, teachers, office mates, fellow officers, and fellow heads of departments, your subordinates or your bosses.

A Myth of a Private Life

So what is the way forward now?

Start behaving properly. Start being careful in whatever you say, whatever you do and the way you live your life. At the end of the day, all these matters.

People are watching, and all these will have a hand on your success.

Private life does not exist. So live as though everyone is watching you.

Get it right, there is no private life. You are not an island. You live with people, and people are watching you.

22

Hired for Attitude

If you are now in secondary school or college or fresh from college and searching for a job, your greatest preparation area should be on your attitude.

The most important fact to remember is that people are hired; more for their attitude and less for their certificates.

I have more than 19 years in the corporate world, and I can assure you that the best performers in the interview room are not those with best college grades but those with the best attitude.

Psychologists define attitude as a learned tendency to evaluate things a certain way. However, the good news is that, according to Viktor E. Frankl, "Our greatest freedom is the freedom to choose our attitude."

My definition of attitude is that it is an emotional feeling that determines the way you will act or react, positively or negatively, to something, someone, a place or situation.

Since you can decide what attitude to carry each day in the same way you decide what cloth to wear, it is up to you. It is your choice.

If you want to have a good future, you need to start training your mind to always carry a progressive attitude. An attitude that will make you want to cooperate with others, enjoy working with people of different backgrounds, people with a different opinion on issues, people that follow different traditions.

I remember in 2001, just a few weeks after being employed by the Habib African Bank, I met a former classmate. He was surprised that I worked with the bank owned by Asians. He had a bad attitude about them because of false prejudices fed into him by his people. The image he had was totally different from what I was experiencing. That incidence made me think. It made me understand why many people fail to grab opportunities that cross their lives just because of bad attitudes built on wrong prejudices.

Such prejudices are found in many aspects of life. They are like bad weeds in the farm, like a bad smell in the air and like mud in the water.

This is why modern companies have adopted a simple policy, hire for attitude and train for skills. Therefore, it is very important at a young age to realize the importance attitude towards your success.

A mind with a positive attitude is like a clean house. The air inside that house is always fresh and living in it is healthy. Likewise, a mind with prejudices is like a dirty house, very unhealthy filled with bad smell. So if you live in a dirty house you will always feel sick whereas if you are in a clean house you will feel good and healthy.

A bad attitude will always lead you into disappointments, conflicts, and stress while good attitude will help you prosper, enjoy yourself and live a life full of success.

21st Century companies are ready to hire a person with right attitude but less skilled than higher a more skilled person with the wrong attitude.

Companies hire people with the right attitude because they know they will be ready to take up challenges and work to their full potential, while people with the wrong attitude will always work just to meet minimum performance and will not be ready to tackle new challenges.

Zig Ziglar said, "Your attitude, not your aptitude, will

Hired for Attitude

determine your altitude." I agree with this guru for 100%. The altitude he is referring to is the level of success in all aspects of your life, be it financially, socially, politically, physiologically and professionally.

My advice to you is start now to feed your mind with positive ideas so that your attitude remains positive all the time.

21st Century companies are ready to hire a person with right attitude but less skilled than higher a more skilled person with the wrong attitude.

23

Sky is Never the Limit

At a very young age, when I started understanding things, I used to think that the highest point in the universe was the sky. These days I still hear people referring to the sky that, "the sky is the limit." I wonder why? When I started my primary school education and attended a geography class I realized that the universe is so huge, that it has no end. As such, whoever stated 'the sky is the limit' phrase must have missed their geography class.

This is what happens with our lives. Sometimes people underestimate their capabilities and tune their minds for low ambitions. As a young person, you have to think big and be always optimistic. Do not allow yourself to be limited by the achievements of your parents or friends. Always seek to break records. Always look at what the best have already achieved and think of ways you can do better. Be it in studies, sports or anything.

Sky is Never the Limit

Sometimes people will ask you who do you want to be in life? It is a normal question, but sometimes we may not have clear answers. Most people will say I want to become a Doctor, or a lawyer, or an accountant but most of the time it is because they have seen some of the family members in those professions. At that point, you may not know the opportunities available for you in the world.

In my case, I have been changing professions as time has gone by because of the situations I was in. Earlier on, I wanted to become an engineer because I had heard that engineers make lots of money and they do not hustle a lot. Being deep in the village I wanted a better life than I was living with my family then. When I joined seminary school I wanted to become a priest. I thought it would have been a cool thing to be because priests live a good life, well respected than anybody in the village. By the time I was in high school I wanted to be a businessman because then I knew, running my own business would give me more money and a much better life. But then I had to go to college and then get employed to get the knowledge that is never taught in school.

Now as I am writing this chapter, I look at myself and wonder that if someone had told me at the age of seven or even at the age of 20 that I would one day become a Speaker, Author, Trainer, and Coach. I would definitely

Ntangeki Nshala

have said NO that is not me, wrong address!

It seems so far totally away from me being a priest to be, an accountant, a banker, a politician, a Rotarian. But in actual fact, who I am today has everything to do with all those. Those paths that I have been through have shaped me to be who I am today. Because when I speak, write, train, mentor or coach I do that based on these past experiences.

My advice to you, whether you are in secondary school or college, is that develop a habit of being the best you can be at what you are doing. If it is about studies, just do your best and break the records. At the same time, you must take some time to discover what you really want to do that makes you happy. You may not know it now or even in five or ten years to come, but keep asking yourself what do I wish to do that really makes me happy doing that I would like to do even for free. When you discover it, do it well, creatively do it uniquely and better than anybody else. After sometime you will be known for it and slowly it will earn you a living, no matter what it is.

Always look at what the best have already achieved and think of ways you can do better.

24

Never Lose your Cool

One cold evening, in Sao Hill Mafinga, while seating in front of our chimney in our living room, I did something that I remember and I regret even after three decades. While I cannot recall what my sister, Advela, did to me, but I know that she annoyed me and without thinking carefully I grabbed her only doll, Subira, and through it into the fire. I must have been around four years old and she must have been six. My sister was and to this day still is a very quiet and peaceful person. On that fateful day, I don't know what went wrong. She cried so much because she loved Subira so much. After a short moment, I felt sorry for her too. I regretted what I had done. My mother gave me a serious beating, but the damage was already done and Subira was gone. I lost my cool, and it cost my sister.

I vividly remember this incident even though I was very young. I remember it because it taught me a lesson. And from that day, I vowed not to react to situations without thinking twice. I learned that without self-control, I could find myself in much bigger problems.

In life, you are 100% sure to find yourself in situations that will annoy you. Your brother or sister may say to you something that will offend you. Your fellow students may do to you something that will trigger your emotions. A total stranger may treat you unfairly. Your parents or teachers may misunderstand you. Your good friends may let you down. Situations may get out of hand and pile pressure on you. You may find yourself under stress with no quick solutions. Many more scenarios may occur to you that will potentially press you to a bursting point. Don't succumb to that pressure. Don't burst. Don't react. Always stay cool, calm and collected.

So goes an old adage, "never make decisions while furious, never make promises when you are happy."

Sometimes the cost of losing your cool can be very high. You can lose your friends, your job, damage your relationship with your loved ones, dent your career, and ruin trust. It can create tensions and cause conflicts in the community. It can be really bad especially when you are wrong.

— *Never lose your Cool* —

People who rise to high positions don't crack under pressure; they coolly think about the situation at hand and handle challenges with wisdom. And they employ skills that work such as persuasiveness, conflict management, they are proactive, and they develop a high level of self-regulation.

You also should prepare yourself for a tough life ahead. Being measured and keeping your cool in all situations is a skill like any other, and so it can be learned and practiced.

One of the questions that you will most likely be asked in job interviews is whether you can work under pressure. This is because the current working environment demands more output and at a shorter time. Hence, mastering this skill from an early age will be very beneficial to you in future.

People who rise to high positions don't crack under pressure; they coolly think about the situation at hand and handle challenges with wisdom.

25

Think

My son, Kiiza, who is now Two and half years old, loves watching cartoons so much so that it has now become difficult to watch other TV programs. Last Sunday, around mid-morning, as I took the remote control to change to my favorite channel, CNBC, Kiiza screamed to the top of his voice as if he had been bitten by a snake. I quickly realized that I had no chance, and so settled for his choice, Disney Junior. A minute or two into watching the cartoon, I was totally captivated by it. Actually, learning a big lesson, Think! The program, My friends Tigger and Pooh, was teaching these young kids to think.

Think, Think, Think! They would sing. What a lesson!

Now, you might not be aware that thinking is a skill like any other. An important skill and unfortunately it is never taught in school. Maybe you are already

Think

wondering what exactly I am talking about because, as a human being you naturally think and need not be taught. My answer to that is Yes and No. Yes, every human being has a certain thinking capacity, and No because the thinking am talking about here is a notch above the normal thinking; I am talking about Creative and Critical thinking.

Relax don't start wondering what these complex words are. They are very simple terminologies. I like simplicity, so I wouldn't like to confuse you, not at all.

Creative thinking is simply the way of looking at a problem, a challenge or a situation from a fresh perspective, not following a common pattern and come with suggestions or solutions that are not traditional or common. Solutions that suggest new ways that sometimes may be unsettling. That is what others call, "thinking outside the box."

In schools and colleges, you are taught to follow what others have already defined. It is a good thing, but not so great. That is how our education system is. It offers you basic knowledge. However good it may be, it is never enough to make you a thinker. Creative thinking is about detaching yourself from the normal ways and independently re-look at a situation at hand and come up with fresh ideas. Your thinking line should always be, "not because many people have been doing it this way, that it is the best way." I can assure you that there is always a better way of doing anything, it is a challenge for you to find out.

Now, if you want to be successful in life, like Diamond Platnumz, Reginald Mengi, Aliko Dangote or Bill Gates you have to learn and apply creative thinking. If you want to shine like a star in any professional field, be it as a doctor, engineer, accountant, banker or lawyer you need not be the most talented but the most creative of all.

Creativity is a mother of success.

Then how do you develop your creative thinking capacity. It is very simple. If you work on the following areas you will go a long way. First, learn a lot about your area of interest, and be good at it. Constantly read books, journals and other current literature about your field. Second, develop a habit of learning new things outside your field by reading widely. This will get you a basic knowledge about other fields like engineering, cooking, human health, sports, military, agriculture, women, men, finance and so on. Thirdly develop self-confidence, and understand that in life you don't have to follow the common path in order to succeed. That something has never been done does not mean it cannot be done. Always avoid biases and unfounded notions but be passionate with facts.

The list is endless, but for me, the last point is for you to bear in mind that you have to overcome the fear of failure. The fear of failure is the number one killer of people's creativity.

If you follow the above few tips, your mind will start looking at things and situations differently. Soon or later you will be constantly searching for alternatives and you will discover new products or solutions to old problems. And that will make you stand out of the rest in your field.

If you wish for success, learn to think creatively.

Let us discuss Critical thinking in our next chapter.

Your thinking line should always be, "not because many people have been doing it this way, that it is the best way."

26

Critical Thinking

Like I said earlier in the previous chapter, thinking is an important skill. More so for youth. The earlier you learn and master it, the better. Critical thinking can be a differentiating factor between the good and the great.

While creative thinking is about finding new ways of doing things, and focusing outwards, critical thinking is about diving in and get to assess the validity of common truth. Therefore, critical thinking is more about verifying the theories that people have been made to believe to be true for a long time in order to gain an insight.

Moore and Parker defined critical thinking as, "The careful application of reason in the determination of whether a claim is true."

This definition has two keywords; care and reason. These carry a lot of meaning individually. So please follow me as I briefly break them down.

Critical Thinking

Careful means you have to be cautious and thorough in analyzing the theory. Look into the details from all possible angles, all parts of the truth. Do not just look at one side and jump into conclusion.

Reason means while analyzing the theory do not be subjective, but always be logical. Logic simply means you follow a rational pattern in arriving at your answer. Do not allow personal emotions to overrule and force you to a conclusion. Logic simply means anyone given same facts will give the same conclusion.

It is very important to master critical thinking skill at an early age. It will give you an edge over many of your peers and above all, it will build in you a strong capability to present your arguments in any conversation.

Critical thinking will help you to always give well thought, logical reasons for your own decisions and those of others. It also helps you own what you believe in instead of simply believing in statements without solid reasons.

I hope you are still with me to this point.

I want to equip you with the single most powerful tool to help you cultivate the power of critical thinking. This tool is what I use every time and every day. Very simple.

Ask questions!

Asking questions has never been a sign of stupidity rather a sign of smartness. It shows that you want to know better and more. Asking questions is a good sign which shows that you are humble too.

But then you have to know what questions to ask, how to ask them and when. If you master these three important aspects you will be unstoppable in learning.

What you have to know is that all knowledge in the world started with questions. When you ask, then you force the other person to think and provide his best answer. However, if you wish to get to the root of his response then you need to pull out your best tool of all. No one has been able to discover a better tool than this. Ask, WHY?

Asking why, is the best learning tool to have been discovered until now. Learn how to use it, and you will have unprecedented success in whatever you do.

Asking why, is the best learning tool to have been discovered until now.

27

Dig Gold Where You Are

I remember my time at St. Mary's Rubya Seminary, where I spent four years of secondary school. It was a tight school. Each day packed with activities. Classes, prayers, sports, manual work and evening study. From morning to evening, no loose time, no free time. By the time I left the school after completing form four, I felt I didn't want to go back there again for High school. God heard my prayers and I was picked for another high school. Now, this is when I realized how good Rubya seminary was. I learned an important lesson in life, that in any situation, waste no time whining, but focus on winning. No wonder the wise said, "Dig gold where you are."

There is gold everywhere. It just depends on what gold is in your situation. Always focus your energy on making the best out of your situation. When you do that, you will gradually realize how much value you can gather even in a place where many people think is a total wasteland.

You might be experiencing the same as I used to during my schooling years. Whether you are in school, college or at work. Do not worry, it is normal. It is human nature to always feel that what we have is not enough and it could have been better. This feeling I believe is natural, because without this inner feeling we would be complacent and never push for the better. However, while dreaming and scheming for a better future, do not let the present pass unutilized.

At a rubbish damping place, there are scavengers searching for something of value. Scavengers are flourishing where others have completely given up and have no hope for anything useful. Fascinating! What if you also develop the mentality of a scavenger? This will be a life-changing mentality. Always to be on the lookout for something useful; ideas or lessons, however bad, useless, hopeless, stressful, awful, terrible the situation or place might be.

A few years back I happened to watch a TV program

Dig Good where you Are

on CNN, just after the 2008 financial crisis in America. They showed a lot of statistics on how people lost their wealth during that period. It was just appalling. Millions of people lost their jobs, homes, businesses, stock investments to mention just a few. Of course, the whole global economy felt the shock waves. But while millions lost, the smart scavengers turned the situation of despair into a super business opportunity and became billionaires during the same period.

Like when I was at Rubya, I always thought the school was not good, too many strict rules, no free time, no outing. In my mind then, every other school could have been better. But now, I know that Rubya is one of the best places to be, and I thank God for having schooled there. It is a pure gold mine in its own right. Everything is gold, the strict school program, the life, education quality, the environment; it is simply an amazing place to be.

This could be the same with your life. The fact that you are not enjoying the situation does not mean it is not enjoyable. It is just your mentality. Change it. The old adage says, "There is a silver lining to every cloud."

Scavengers are not overwhelmed by the status of the garbage because they are focused on searching for value in it. You too, should not allow your mind to be overwhelmed by your life stresses, difficulties or challenges, but focus your mind and energy on identifying the few positives and make the most of the situation.

Wherever you are, there is a value; there is gold, dig it!

Scavengers are not overwhelmed by the status of the garbage because they are focused on searching for value in it.

28

Biija Mpola

I couldn't find exact words to translate this Kihaya saying, but the closest would be, "things come slowly." Maybe putting it into context one would say, "There is no overnight success." I hope we are on the same page now.

You might be wondering why I am writing about this topic. It is pretty much common sense. Oh yes, I know, it is common sense, but it is not common practice. It is even more so for those in schools and colleges.

It is a fact of life that we showcase fine products for the world to see, admire and maybe purchase. When you walk downtown, you see shops full of very nice, beautiful, polished products. All placed ready for you to use, very valuable products. When you like what you see, you make a purchase. That is how we operate. Showrooms are always neat; well designed, beautifully decorated and brightly lit. Everything in the showroom looks just stunning. That is why for any purchase you have to pay a premium. This is our way of life and it works well for all.

Come to think of it, no one showcases a workshop. Maybe because no one is interested in looking at the dirty work that goes on behind the closed doors. But if you want to appreciate the value of the final product it would make a lot of sense to learn what it truly takes to have the magnificent final product.

At a young age, you may wish to become successful in your life. Whatever kind of success is possible in this world. You may wish to become as successful as Diamond Platnumz, Bakhresa, Dangote, Bill Gates, Barrack Obama, Christiano Ronaldo, Floyd Mayweather and the like. It is possible. I too wish that you have dreams so big that you even want to surpass these champions. It is possible. It can be done. There is only one simple requirement to become the best you wish to be. That requirement is, to be willing to do what it takes. It is that simple! Just willingness to do whatever it will require.

Get me right. I say, it is simple, but I am not saying it is easy. It is simple because you do not require rocket science to decide to follow your dream to the end.

However, it is not easy because it will require a lot of resources mainly time, energy and money. To become a champion, you will require many years of hard work and will call for a lot of sacrifices along the way. You have to be ready to shed your blood, sweat, and tears.

Above all, it takes time. You have to be willing to wait, because true success comes slowly, gradually, step by step. There is no overnight success like some people think. Those you see in the lime light have spent countless hours in the dark corners working. The champions you see on television have spent years and years working on their skills. They are standing on the world stage today after many years on their knees working on their dreams. It is not that they made that decision yesterday.

If you look around you will see some people who are already getting serious on their dreams. This reminds me of my school friend and classmate, Gerald Mutarubukwa. He was one of the smartest people I have ever seen. For six years, that is from standard six to form four, he was always the first in class in all monthly exams we ever did. Now I understand the secret of his success. He had developed and mastered the habit of working hard. I don't remember seeing him playing around or hearing him making noise in class or during personal study periods. He had a very high sense of focus and concentration on studies. His performance mirrored his efforts. No wonder, it is said, "hard work pays."

Take home is, life is like a mirror, it gives you back the equivalent of what you put in. So, an extraordinary effort will yield extraordinary results and poor efforts for poor results.

Success is for those who are willing to succeed no matter what. If you want your future to be big and great, start now with small acts in a great way. The earlier you start the better because it requires time to reach the top.

To become a champion, you will require many years of hard work and will call for a lot of sacrifices along the way. You have to be ready to shed your blood, sweat, and tears.

29

In Rome, Be a Roman

This old adage carries a lot of wisdom, "When in Rome, do what Romans do." It must have been relevant then, but I find it much more relevant now.

If there is one quality that will play a huge role for success in the 21st century, then it will be an ability to be multicultural. The world has truly turned into a global village. People are connected so much so that everything has become global. It now takes just a few minutes for information to move from one angle of the world to another. Actually more and more events now are streamed live. It used to be TV but the internet has revolutionalized everything.

Traveling around the world has become easier and cheaper and many businesses have become global. Mid May 2017, I was in Fatima Portugal, attending the canonization ceremony of the two shepherds, Francisco and Jacinta. There were a lot of people from all over the world. I met people from Spain, Angola, DRC, Brazil, Italy, and Portugal. As I moved around the Fatima shrine, during the ceremony and in restaurants all people mingled freely without worries. It was a convergence of over a million people, all seeing each other as family.

Movement of capital and labor keep getting easier as each day goes by. Opportunities are no longer local and business competition is now international. Darwin's law of nature, "survival of the fittest" comes into play. If you have to survive and thrive you have to be among the best. The average and common will be shelved, treated like a commodity, never to realize their true value.

Where do you want to belong? The fittest, I presume.

The fittest will have to be multicultural. Success in this era will need you to be among those who can work, live, eat, drink, dance, and communicate with other people regardless of their culture, color, faith, or background.

Adapting well to other people's culture will give you a lot of advantages such as making you feel confident and secure when dealing with people from a different background. Feeling confident will boost your ability to connect and achieve your goals with those people, be it social or business.

— *In Rome, Be a Roman* —

Being multicultural will avail the opportunity to benefit from the best from others. Meaning that you will learn how others deal with situations that you face too. Your ability to pull knowledge from various areas will make you think creatively in problem-solving.

Recently I was engaged in a conversation with my young brother whose work demands him to travel to many countries. He told me that early in his career while attending an international meeting in West Africa, a panelist caught the attention of many on how she could eloquently present her arguments both English and French. He said the way she switched languages captivated many, and her arguments became well understood. This story underscores the power of being multicultural.

Apart from all those benefits and many others that one can get by being adaptable to other people's cultures, the greatest of all is the capacity to expand your network. In the business world, the greatest asset apart from capital and staff is the network. Now if you have a network of people who know and trust you from various backgrounds, it increases your possibility of expanding your business and making it more bigger and better.

In that regard, regardless of your current age, whether

you are in school, college or working, always appreciate the power of being multicultural and look for opportunities to learn and network with people from different backgrounds.

Success in this era will need you to be among those who can work, live, eat, drink, dance, and communicate with other people regardless of their culture, color, faith, or background.

— *Ntangeki Nshala* —

30

Education is Key

25th May 2017, Mark Zuckerberg was awarded an honorary doctorate by Harvard University, 12 years after dropping out from the same college. Today, the founder of Facebook is one of the richest people in the world. Bill Gates, now presumed to be the richest person in the world, also a Harvard University dropout, after 30 years returned to Harvard in June 2007 to collect his honorary doctorate. These are two most recognized college dropouts who have defied the odds and went on to be super successful with their dreams. Looks confusing. A college dropout and yet the most successful!

It gets many people asking themselves whether education matters. If Bill Gates, Mark Zuckerberg and many others could drop out and become what they are today, then why waste time in schools and colleges. Why not go out there and face the world head on and hopefully come our victorious like Bill and Mark? Yet these two represent hundreds of successful people in the world who never had an opportunity to attend universities.

So why is formal education important? This must be one of many questions that keep knocking on your mind.

But let me shed a little light here, when did Mark Zuckerberg and Bill Gates drop out? The answer is simple in college. Harvard! What does this mean? It means these people were super smart and lucky. These two elements don't match very often. And if you look deeper, these two went to best schools from early on.

Besides, these two dropped out of college to pursue something they had already figured out, and they had skills to initialize it to some meaningful level. They were prepared.

So what is the lesson here? Education is important.

I look at formal education as a base or a foundation on which a house is built. When you are well educated, it means your foundation is strong enough to carry any building however tall. When you are not so much educated it means you have a weak foundation which can only manage small, light structures. So what does that mean, it simply means a well-educated person can handle much bigger and complex tasks than a less

Education is Key

educated one.

Get me right. I look at education from ability side and not a number of certificates. I want you also, to change your mind and build your ability. If you are in secondary school or college focus your energy on understanding what teachers give. Seek to understand because that is when you can use the knowledge and create your own product. Unfortunately, many students just swallow whatever teachers say. They don't really bother to get the full picture. They are lazy. Do not be one of them, be above them.

It never ceases to amaze me when I meet college graduate seeking to join the labor market but can hardly express themselves in a well structured meaningful sentence. Some, six months down the line, cannot properly respond to a basic question regarding their college major. And yet these will show you a nice CV and certificates.

Sad! The labor market requires people with an ability to produce, no one cares about certificates. I am writing this book to help you, and so if you have to take only one lesson from this book, then note that education is more about building your ability and much less about certificates.

If your certificates do not match with your ability, soon or later you will be thrown out of the labor market. I have been in the corporate world for more than 17 years, and so I am talking from solid experience.

So stop scheming to pass exams, study to understand and empower your mind, so that when you are out of college you are able to survive and thrive in the labor market and in your business ventures.

I look at formal education as a base or a foundation on which a house is built. When you are well educated, it means your foundation is strong enough to carry any building however tall.

31

Talent is Never Enough

I am a football fan. I follow three different football clubs from three different leagues. In the Tanzania's Ligi Kuu I am a Yanga fan, in the English Premier League I am a Chelsea fan and in La Liga, I am a Real Madrid fan. Generally, I like sports. For a long time, I have been following tennis and I have been fascinated by Star legends like Pete Sampras, Andre Agas, Steffi Graff and the current stars like the Williams sisters, Andy Murray and Novak Djokovic. I like Tiger Woods in golf and Lewis Hamilton in Formula One. I follow athletics, boxing, and basketball. In short, I am a sports fan.

Although I draw a lot of personal enjoyment and happiness from these sports, I have come to realize that I am now drawing important life lessons as well. One of them is on talent.

Naturally, players become stars because sports competitions are watched by many and a lot of emotions is involved. And also because a lot of money is involved best talents are attracted to best teams. In recent years we have witnessed talented players like Lionel Messi and Christiano Ronaldo. These two are the finest for now. They have dominated the football world and receive a lot of team prizes and personal prizes. They are a very good example of the best combination of talent and discipline.

On the other hand, when talent does not meet discipline or self-awareness the outcome is financial loss and personal disappointment. This happens in sports as well as in our everyday life.

I believe if you are in school or college, or even you are now out of college, you can still remember your years there, there are always students who are never serious with studies. They are normally trouble makers, noise makers with never ending drama. However, despite all those issues, they are among the top performers in the class. For them, passing exams comes with just little efforts.

They remind me of Mario Balotelli in football. An

Talent is Never Enough

Italian super talent. At age 18 he was billed to be one of the most promising players in the world. He was said to be a complete striker, height, physic, footwork, and smartness. He was a rare talent. All big clubs admired Inter Milan who had him then. To the contrary, Balotelli turned out to be a total disappointment. One main reason is lack of discipline.

Many talents have been wasted in the same way, in all professions, all over the world. Many reasons can be attributed to those failures but other than physical accidents, lack of discipline comes to the top.

Like I said in our school classes, those talented students who refuse to work hard normally end up with life much below their potential. Some students join the college with very nice passes from high school but fail to shine in college, because of lack of discipline and self-management. They get carried out and lose focus.

Therefore, if you know you are talented in a certain area, do not be complacent. Success comes more with hard work and less with talent. But if you will maintain a composed mind, and build a capability to match hard work with your talent, then be sure of extraordinary results.

All successful people work hard, Ronaldo and Messi

work hard. Aliko Dangote, Reginald Mengi, Mohamed Dewji and many others, all work very hard. They put in the hours! They work hard. Hard work beats talent when talent fails to work hard.

Once again I repeat, if you want to have success in your life, then you have to always remember that, talent is not enough.

Hard work beats talent when talent fails to work hard.

32

Kindness Matters

When I think of kindness I can't help but remember a very touching story that I recently came across in social media. A now, very senior government officer in South Africa, gave an account of how he approached Asian trader in his small town seeking for a loan so as to assist his mother and siblings while he attends university. Mr. Musa, the Asian trader, after listening to this desperate young man, agreed to give a loan, not in cash but allowed the mother to collect monthly groceries from the shop. All these were done with no written contract, just words. Three years after university, the gentleman turns up at Mr. Musa's shop for a repayment arrangement and the answer he gets is, "nothing to pay, go do the same to others."

What an act of kindness! It is just unbelievable how people can be so kind. What Mr. Musa did to this gentleman is exactly what Jesus said, "do to others as you would like them to do to you."

Kindness is about being nice, generous and considerate to others. You don't need to have a reason to be kind; it is something you do because it is the right way to treat others. Kind people do not do kind acts expecting a return but they do it because they feel it is the right thing.

You don't have to be Mr. Musa to be kind. You can show kindness in your everyday life and make a big difference in other people's lives. Surprisingly the acts of kindness you do make you happy too. That's the major benefit of kindness.

By now you might be wondering what is it that you can do to be kind. Relax, kindness is seen in very little acts but it has a huge and long lasting impact to people. Like what Maya Angelou said, "I have learned that people will forget what you said, people will forget what you did, but people will never forget how you made them feel."

This takes me to another example that I read a long time back, about a lady working at a factory. For many years she would come to work in the morning and leave in the evening like any other employee. One evening while closing her work, as part of a routine, she entered

Kindness Matters

the cold room where they stored frozen food, and by mistake, the door shut and there was no way one could open from inside. Since the room was sealed no one could hear her voice, and so she sat in there, helpless, hopeless waiting to freeze to death. After one hour or so, someone opens the door, and it was the watchman. Happy and thankful for the miracle, the lady became curious as to how the watchman came in office, that was not part of his job. Then the watchman responded, "For all years I have worked here, it is only you who greets me in the morning and wishes me goodbye in the evening. So when I did not see you leave the office, I sensed something must have gone wrong, and I decided to check around."

Wow! I hope now you understand the power of kindness.

When you have cultivated the habit of kindness, you do kind things unknowingly, because that is how you are. These acts come naturally to you. They seem common sense and you do them effortlessly. Naturally, human beings like to pay kindness for kindness. Although kind people don't do expecting payback, kindness comes back to them unknowingly too.

There are countless simple acts of kindness like; smiling to a stranger, genuinely compliment people, congratulate friends for good accomplishments, donate time, things or money, say Thank You, say Please, assist a stranger, hold a door for others, be compassionate to others, don't judge, put yourself in other people's shoes, and so on. The list can never be exhausted.

What you have to remember is that memories of simple acts of kindness are stored in people's hearts. That is why they last a lifetime. People may not talk about it, may not know how to express it, but will always feel it inside.

While kindness is mostly about you doing for others, you also need to be kind to yourself. There are many ways to show kindness to yourself like; forgive yourself for not being what you should have been in the past. Learn a lesson and plan to make future better. Give yourself a break from stressful life and engage in things that make you happy. Appreciate yourself for your accomplishments.

Kindness may be a soft skill that yields lifelong results. Master it!

"I have learned that people will forget what you said, people will forget what you did, but people will never forget how you made them feel." – Maya Angelou -

33

Exercise is Power

During my secondary school years, sports used to be one of the never miss activities. I was so passionate about sports, but that is not the whole truth. The truth is that there was no choice. In my school, sports were a must for everyone, every day, unless you are sick and so you have a special permission from the teachers. At Rubya, sports were a big deal. Dodging sports could cost you dearly.
I enjoyed playing basketball. It was my favorite. I liked the intensity and physical fitness it demanded. It left me with a lot of good memories.

So while I enjoyed the games, I could not link it with academic performances. Now that I have read about many types of research, I have come to fully appreciate the importance of sports and understand why my school made it mandatory for every student, every day.

Recently I was reading the Harvard Health Publications issued by the Harvard Medical School. It said that a research was done and proved that regular exercise changes the brain to improve memory and thinking skills. The article said, "In a study done at the University of British Columbia, researchers found that regular aerobic exercise, the kind that gets your heart and your sweat glands pumping, appears to boost the size of the hippocampus, the brain area involved in verbal memory and learning."

These could be only a few out of many benefits of physical exercise such as; reduce the possibility of heart diseases, stroke, and diabetes. Keep yourself young and strong, reduce body weight and prevent depression. Benefits of physical exercise are many.

Many schools and colleges these days do not care much about sports. Some do not even have sports grounds and many others do not put much emphasis on sports. But it is the students that suffer. You may not see it directly, but you are paying the cost silently.

My simple advice to you, in whatever situation you may be in if there are slim opportunities of exercising, use them fully. Engage in any kinds of sports that will engage your body and make you sweat.

—— *Exercise is Power* ——

When you are at home, find time to exercise. Now, you might think that you have to enroll yourself in the gym and maybe you do not have the fees. You do not have to. I am not a member of any gym. I make it very simple. I exercise at home. There are many exercises that can be performed even at your bedside. So you do not have any excuses, whatsoever, for not doing physical exercises.

On the other hand, if you engage in many physical activities at home, then you may not need intense exercises.

Just imagine, a President of the United States of America has a mandatory schedule of exercising. It is said that the kind of office work that he carries in a day is so stressful so much so that an unfit body will easily collapse. In that regard, for the president, exercise and fitness are a matter of national security. What about you and me?

At a young age, you might not appreciate the importance of this matter, may be because you are fit and you do not feel any kind of sickness. And, maybe you want to wait until you grow gray hair to start exercising. Wrong! That might be too late.

My humble advice to you is, start now, and start today.

Do not think that because you are young you are safe

from diseases like; high and low blood pressure, heart diseases, stroke, and diabetes. There already is a growing trend of young people getting a stroke. So no one is safe. The only preventive measure is keeping yourself fit.

"...a research was done and proved that regular exercise changes the brain to improve memory and thinking skills." – Harvard Medical School -

---

34

Live Legally

I admire the men and women in uniforms, the soldiers. They are meticulous about what they do. They have been trained to live a life very different from civilians. They live by rules, regulations, and orders. They cherish seniority and I guess that is their number one rule. Obedience of rules and laws is what keeps all armies intact. Armies can carry very huge, challenging and wide operations under a leadership of only one person. But how do they manage to do this? The answer is straightforward, abiding by the laws.
We are civilians, but we can learn from our brothers and sisters in the armed forces. Live by the law, live legally.

It is a fact of life that a large percentage of people in our jails is young people who have been caught being on the wrong side of the law. These people were not born with bad habits; they just learned them here on earth. In our streets. Actually, some have learned them in schools.

One important point to note is that bad habits don't just happen. They are developed over time. They start small, and if not reprimanded, they keep growing, and after some time they become unmanageable and dangerous.

Like I said, these guys in jails were once as nice as you are. They also were smart, humble, innocent and with big dreams. But somehow, somewhere, bad ideas were planted into their minds, and slowly they practiced them and later turned out to be criminals.

Sometimes, these bad habits may be hidden and the law may not catch up with you until much later in your life when you are a very grown up person. But you can be sure, that one day, you will be caught.

In order to escape these traps, and temptations of breaking the laws it is important to start now living by them. Start now when you are still young. Train your mind to follow all rules and laws however small. It does not matter you are in secondary school, college or already working. Train yourself to abide by all rules even when no one cares, when no one is watching, or no one can punish you. As long as it is a rule or law, just obey it.

I understand that in schools and colleges there is always a mob psychology. Groups tend to motivate people to

Live Legally

break the law. Some people might start discouraging you and think you are a fool. Just ignore them. Their mob psychology makes them think they are smarter, simply because they were never caught breaking the law or they were never punished. That is fine. But the fact is, they have planted within them a seed of disobedience, and because it is taking time to be noticed, it will grow and the price they will pay will be very high.

I can't thank my school teachers enough. The obedience they inculcated in us while in school has been a strong shield in today's life challenges. Our school used to be like an army camp. There were lots of rules and regulations, and any misstep used to be heavily punished, if not discontinued. I used to think it was too harsh, but now I understand.

I am sharing with you a very important life lesson. Living legally is not a simple matter. I have seen people getting frustrated in offices because of their failure to follow simple rules. Some people are not promoted and some even get dismissed from work because of constant failure to abide by the rules and regulations. They get frustrated. They do not understand why things are happening to them. But I can assure you, the root of the problem starts when they were young, in secondary schools and colleges. At the point they are already grownups, changing bad habits becomes a huge challenge. The cost becomes very high. They suffer and their families suffer too.

Please save yourself from these pains. Start now. Develop a habit of abiding by rules and regulations. Love to live legally always.

Train yourself to abide by all rules even when no one cares, when no one is watching, or no one can punish you.

35

Set Goals

Once in a while, I drive from Dar es Salaam to my village in Muhutwe, Muleba. This is about 1,500 kilometers. It is a very long, tiring journey. It makes me feel exhausted body and mind. Over time I discovered a technique that I use to make this long journey seem easy and enjoyable. It is a simple mind technique. I divide the whole journey into six short journeys and after everyone, there is a brief stop for breakfast, lunch or stretching. So it would be Dar to Morogoro, Morogoro to Dodoma, Dodoma to Singida, Singida to Nzega, Nzega to Kahama, and then Kahama to Muhutwe. So when I start in Dar, I don't think much of Muhutwe but rather I focus on reaching Morogoro. To these are my milestones, my goals.

Every long journey needs milestones. Milestones will keep you focused and will remind you that you are still on the right track. Without milestones, you might get lost. That is also the reason why engineers put signposts on the highway showing how many kilometers or miles to reach a certain destination.

What milestones do to highway travelers, so do goals to your life dreams. So goals are milestones to your dreams. You have to drive to achieve them. When you complete one goal you start another one until you reach your dream destination.

There are destinations that people take in life. For example, different people may follow different careers. Some want to be engineers, doctors, bankers, accountants, lawyers, teachers, soldiers, and so on. All these are career journeys.

You might be many students in the same class, but everyone has her or his own destination. Depending on your destination, emphasis on subjects or courses may differ. Let us say you are in Ordinary Level and dream to become a doctor, then from early on you have to love science subjects especially biology, goals number one will be to pass well in form four so that you qualify for high school probably for PCB (Physics, Chemistry, Biology). The second goals will be pass form six with good grades to join Muhimbili University or any other

— Set Goals —

Health Sciences University in the world.

While in university your third goal is to go through the first year, the second year…and so on.

The same applies for those who want to become whatever they wish to become. The formula is the same, plan short term actions that will lead to the big dream.

Don't sit and expect things just to happen. Nothing happens until someone does something. For your life and for your dreams, that someone is you. Do something.

Goals do not have to take years; you can break them into daily, weekly, monthly, semi-annually or yearly activities.

While you set your goals, remember a simple formula that each goal has to abide by. It is known as SMART meaning; Specific, Measurable, Attainable, Relevant and Timed.

A specific goal means it is clear to you. Not vague. Whoever reads it gets the same meaning. For example in a school situation; pass Physics, Chemistry, and Biology with "A"s in my June terminal exams. It is specific because you have named the targeted subjects.

Measurable means your goal has indicators that show

progress of implementation. In this example; your goal is measured by pass grades. There are many grades; A, B, C, D etc and you have targeted an A.

Attainable means with enough efforts you can achieve it. Also because whatever is needed to achieve is available. You need to put challenging targets, not those that are easy to achieve. It does not need to have been attained by others before, maybe you will be the first to reach that high. In this example; getting straight "A"s in all three subjects could be the most challenging.

Relevant means that it has to be leading you to your final destination. In this example; we assume you want to become a Doctor, in that regard if you are in Ordinary level the three subjects are the most relevant. I am not in any way that other subjects should be ignored, not at all. Always follow teacher's instruction, but have goals in your mind.

Timed; in this example, the time comes when you say, June terminal exams. They say a goal without a time limit is just a wish. In this case, we are fine because our time is June. Not December, not next year, not next month, it is June terminal exams.

Setting up your goals by following this simple formula will help you stay focused.

Set Goals

The bonus point is that, write your goals down. Writing is magical. When you take your pen to write your goals down, you will be forced to think again about the goal and get it clearer. As you write it down on paper, it gets written in your mind too. Your mind will mirror it. If you don't write it, it will be vague and forgotten after a short time.

So goals are milestones to your dreams. You have to drive to achieve them. When you complete one goal you start another one until you reach your dream destination.

36

Fluent in Finance

About 10 years ago my good friend Dunstan Kaijage gave me a very valuable present. I met Dustan while attending the CPA review classes around 1997. We got along very well and since then we have been good friends, so are our wives and children. Dunstan new my love for books, and so he gave me a book for a present. It was a Robert Kiyosaki masterpiece, Rich Dad, Poor Dad.
Being an accountant, the book was easy to understand. In this book, Kiyosaki is challenging the traditional definitions and put across his point of view in a superb manner. No wonder the book continues to be on demand until today.

If there is only a message to take away from the book, then it is the importance of becoming financial fluent from a young age.

Although some people preach that money is bad, evil and a product of a devil, there is no way we can escape and underestimate the importance of money in our lives. Actually, we have to work hard to earn every cent. So, we better educate ourselves on how best to handle money, so that we can understand its language, earn enough of it and so attain financial freedom.

The earlier you adopt the culture and master the language of finance the better. That is why I am writing this for you believing at this young age you will develop interest and join the tribe of financial fluent people.

See, from a young age, since my days in primary school, I was always curious to know how people become rich. Obviously, it is because I grew up in a very low-income family in the village. Throughout my secondary school life, I never came across any training that talked about money. My curiosity lived in me for many years until the day of Epiphany.

My epiphany came one Saturday morning when Deus, my distant cousin, came home for a visit. I had not met him for two years or so. As we were catching up with each other, he mentioned to me about his accounting studies. That short conversation changed my life. He didn't know, but he had answered my lifelong curiosity.

I immediately changed my plans of joining a medical college and went on to become an accountant. Everyone thought I was crazy, but I have never regretted my decision.

It is not that you also need to drop your dreams to become an accountant like me, not at all. But I want you to know that, learning how money is made and how best to manage it and multiply it is what differentiates the rich and the poor. You need to be on the winning side, the rich side.

Earlier on, I had always thought money can only be made by accountants, I was dead wrong. The truth is that, there is money everywhere. If you become an engineer, doctor, banker, teacher, lawyer, architect, auditor, soldier you can still make money and become rich. What you require is understanding how to make money in your profession and how to multiply it in the market.

Almost all of us make money or are presented with opportunities to make money, but the problem remains, how do we deal with it when we have it, or how do we deal with the opportunities when we meet them.

At this point, what matters is not the level of education you will be having, the number of "A"s on your certificates, but the attitude in your mind. That is why there is always a debate as to why "A" students end up working for "C" students. To which my honest opinion is the attitude in dealing with money and opportunities that come with it.

Let me share with you some tips that will help you start developing simple financial management techniques;

Savings; whenever you are given some pocket money do not use it all to the last cent. Always save some, like 10% or more for future use. Even if you have not planned what to buy yet, just save.

Be frugal; if you have to spend your money, then make sure that you really need that item you are buying. See, most people buy 'stuff'. These are things that are nice, cheap but of no much use. Therefore before making any spending ask yourself, "Is it not possible to live without it?"

Budget; from today you can start to budget for your money before spending. This will help you spend your money on items you seriously need and eliminate ad hoc spending based on others influence.

Multiply; make your money produce more money. Now, this used to be a challenge when I was growing up in school, but not now. If you are still in school or college you might not have time to run a business, but you can place your money in a bank account that earns interest. Better still you can invest in a stock market, which is my favorite. Stocks are the best because you can start with any amount, however small.

Those are just a few, but the main point is that you need to know that wise use of the money that come to you is what will define the level of your success. It is not the amount of money that comes to you but the skill to handle the money that matters.

…learning how money is made and how best to manage it and multiply it, is what differentiates the rich and the poor.

37

A Wolf in a Pack

June 3rd, 2017, my favorite football team, Real Madrid, was crowned the champion of Europe for the historical 12th time. It was just a fantastic match played in Cardiff, Wales. Cristiano Ronaldo led the scoring and made it to 600 career goals. People are now divided on who is currently the best player in the world; is it Ronaldo or Messi. For sure this is a never ending debate, and it might take a long time to be resolved as the two players are still taking turns to win trophies.

While understanding the individual contribution these two players make in winning trophies, the fact of the matter is that, at the end of the day, it is a team performance that makes the difference. Ronaldo or Messi alone can do nothing.

It is Team Work!

I love the statement from Rudyard Kipling in The Jungle

Book which says, "The strength of the Pack is the Wolf and the strength of the Wolf is the Pack."

He summarized it superbly well.

But Michael Jordan, the legendary basketball star said it well too, "Talent wins games, but teamwork and intelligence win championships."

The lesson is very clear here. No matter how talented you might be, you need to collaborate with others to achieve great results. It is a fact of life that no one has the ability to do everything by him or herself.

Always results that can be achieved by a team are much better than individual results summed up together. This means that when people work individually, there is a lot they lose in the process. No wonder the old adage says, unity is power.

If you have seen wolves hunt, then you know how they can be a great example what teamwork truly looks like. It is amazing how these animals organize themselves. Wolves are neither the fastest, nor the biggest in the jungle, but they attack huge animals like buffalos and rhinos. A lone wolf can't dare attach a rhino, least he gets killed.

― *A Wolf in a Pack* ―

Now, you might be wondering how to apply this knowledge in a school or college setting. It is true that in schools and colleges results are measured by exams pass grades, and exams are done by each one alone. That is fine. But in this setting, collaboration comes during preparations. During personal studying time.

While in school and in college I lent that during group discussions the person who tries to share his or her understanding on a particular subject gains too. It is magical. It is like a training ground. When you stand to present to a group you get a chance to affirm your understanding and in case you had some gaps, members will point them out and help you find a solution. In that case, it is a win - win situation.

In a corporate setting, there are teams too. For the company to achieve its goals, all departments must collaborate with each other. People in administration, operations, marketing, finance, audit, risk, and others have to have the same goal in mind.

You must have heard of brainstorming. This is a meeting where people come together to share ideas on how to tackle a problem at hand. It is a session where no one knows the exact solution but in the process of thinking aloud and suggesting possible options, team members connect, merge or modify vague suggestions and produce the right solution.

You need to take note that, although teamwork is a very good idea, winning demands each member plays their role well. Teamwork never meant being lazy and hiding behind others. For a team to win, the weakest link will be thrown out or replaced. Make sure it is not you. Therefore in a team, individual performance matters a lot.

"Talent wins games, but teamwork and intelligence win championships." – Michael Jordan -

---

38

The Power of Words

"Do not let any unwholesome talk come out of your mouths, but only what is helpful for building others up according to their needs, that it may benefit those who listen" (Ephesians 4:29).

Words when pronounced articulately at the right time to the right audience can change people's lives for better or for worse.

Words are powerful. They can heal or kill.

When Tanzania declared war with Uganda in the 70s, Mwl. Julius Nyerere, the President of United Republic Tanzania gave an emotional speech in which he said, "We have the will, have the reason and we have the capability..." These words moved the whole nation and every citizen rallied behind him and supported the war.

Nyerere's words helped to save the country which was invaded by the Ugandan soldiers.

On the other side, the infamous Hitler, the leader of Germany, was a great speaker who ruled his country and used word power to convince Germans to go to war. By the power of Hitler's words, millions of lives were lost.

You might not be Nyerere or Hitler, but the power of words has never diminished. Actually, with better communication channels, the impact of words can be global.

But I want you to focus this matter at a personal level. Words can be your best tool towards success, but at the same time, your words can be your worst nightmare.

Your words tell the world who you really are, for the mouth speaks what the heart is full of. If you have a kind heart, peaceful and loving your words will be nice, pleasant and friendly. But if your heart is full of jealousy, hate, and malice your words will be harsh, unforgiving and intolerant.

Since God has created with this single most powerful tool the world has ever had, you have the obligation to use it properly with the intention to help others live better.

When in debates or any other discussions, chose your words well. Presenting your points with right words may matter more than the point itself.

The Power of Words

Your ability to use the right words, in a right way, at the right time with the right audience can make you a great person and will open doors for you.

Never use words to belittle others, or show you are superior to others. Always speak in a manner that shows respect and honesty. Truth does not warranty you to be harsh. Be polite even when you differ in opinion with the person you are talking to.

Don't speak when you are furious. Anger can make you speak words you will live to regret.

Minding your words does not mean that you should not speak, but rather be watchful of every word that goes from your mouth because you will never retrieve it back.

In order to be safe with your words, you need to clear your thoughts first. if your mind is full of peace, love, and respect then you are sure any word that will come out any time will reflect it. So, be careful with what you feed your mind. Filter what you read and what you listen to. We live in a century where we are constantly bombarded with information from left, right, and center. We have radios, TV, books, Smartphones, and Computers. All these feed us information.

See, your mind cannot resist the temptation of believing

something that is consistently presented to it. So, consistent positive information will fill your mind with positivity, and negative information will fill your mind with negativity.

On the other hand, your words become your actions. In that regard, if your words are bad and negative your actions will be filled with trouble. If your words are positive, then your actions will be a blessing to all around you.

If you want a prosperous and happy life, start with your words. Be mindful of every word from your mouth, and you will be safe.

Words when pronounces articulately at the right time to the right audience can change people's lives for better or for worse.

39

Who is your Role Model

Role models are people that we admire for their achievements. Their success inspires us. We like to grow up to become like them. We might be close to them or not, it doesn't matter. The most important thing about role models is that we have information about them and we are motivated to follow their steps and have the same level of success or even more.

My role model in business has been Mr. Reginald Mengi, the Chairman of IPP group of companies. He inspires me. And this came naturally when I first heard about him, in the early 90s. I have since known many successful people in business and other professional careers, but Mr. Reginald Mengi is still my number one.

Ntangeki Nshala

When I look at him, I see the future me.

There are two or more qualities that I share with Mengi. One, he is a professional accountant like me and secondly, he has a strong entrepreneurial spirit which has led to his successes, and I feel the same. I might not venture into the same kind of businesses as him, but I believe principals are the same. Above all, he has a big heart of helping those less privileged, which I share the same in many ways. I help many people in villages, and also as a Rotarian, I volunteer in many community development projects. Not for money or fame, but for humanity.

To me, Reginald Mengi is a good role model because he lives and operates in my environment. He is local. Of course, it would have been great to meet him and get to know him better. I believe, one day I will have that opportunity.

Now, who is your role model?

Do you even have any? I know you might be thinking, my father, or my mother! That can be fine too. If your father or your mother has achieved a very high level of success that inspires you to achieve the same, that is fine. However, most of us want to achieve much more

Who is your Role Model

than what our parents have been able to.

Role models come in different types. When I was in secondary school, I admired those who were in high school and I wanted to be like them. Pass my form four national exams like them. Those were my role models. Now that I am a family man, there are other people with families that I admire and want to lead my family like them. They are my role models in that area.

If you are in college, you are already specializing in a certain course. Do you know people who have excelled in that field? Do they inspire you to professionally grow to their level or beyond?

Sometimes you get inspired by people who struggled and later triumphed against problems that are similar to what you are currently facing.

Role models are very important in any aspect of your life. They help you measure your position or progress with the best in that area. If something cannot be measured, it cannot be improved. So is your potential. You will get improvements in trying to close the gap between you and your role model.

So, if at the moment you do not have a role model, do not feel strange. It is ok. But then from now start looking into yourself, assess your current situation and look at people you would like to be like. You might find them within your family, or neighborhood, church, school or workplace.

Also, you might find inspirational people in books. It is ok. Like me, when it comes to family life, I am very much inspired by Barrack Obama. You also might find inspiration from far away.

It is a challenge to get appropriate role models in some environments where people don't write about their lives. It becomes difficult to know people and their secret of success.

Whatever the case, find your role model. Get inspired. Push your limits!

Do you know people who have excelled in that field? Do they inspire you to professionally grow to their level or beyond?

40

A Drop of Greatness

Guinness beer is known for their great TV commercials. One caught my attention most. A football scout gets picked by a taxi driver and goes to a training ground to watch players train. The ball comes to where he was standing with his driver. The driver picks it, plays with it and shows much greater talent than players inside the field. It then says, "There is a drop of greatness in every man."

I agree with them 100%. In every person, there is a hidden talent. Waiting to be uncovered polished and developed. When that is done, it can produce a lot of value.

I believe, God has placed a treasure in you too.

Your biggest challenge is to identify your treasure and work on it to make it valuable in the market.

Many talents reveal to us in the form of hobbies, or things we can do effortlessly. No wonder many people overlook their talents and go around looking for careers that end up frustrating them.

In school, talents can be seen very easily. There are those who love certain subjects and seem to understand everything to do them without much effort. While others struggle to grasp simple principles about it.

I am a perfect example, while in form one and two my performance used to be very average, always in the second half. At that time no one would have believed that in national form four exams I would emerge among the best in class. But I did.

Now, you might be struggling with science subjects but very good in arts subjects, its normal. Maybe mathematics causes nightmares to you, you are not alone. Maybe you like sports more than class works, do not worry, you might be the next Messi or Ronaldo.

No one lacks talent. Every person is talented.

There are few methods that you can use to know your talents. One of the ways is to ask. Ask friends to tell you what they think your talents are. Ask many people so that you reduce the percentage of biased responses.

A Drop of Greatness

You can also look at the subjects that you like the most in your conversations. What are topics that you like to discuss the most? Topics that you are more passionate about. This might give you a direct answer or drop a hint which leads to the right answer.

Also look at activities that you like doing, and don't bore you however long to engage in them. These could be your real talent. Hobbies can be talents or hints to a hidden talent.

Now, all these are easier said than done. Finding your talent is not easy. You have to be patient and always searching. Your greatness will come when you find something that you can easily do and you are passionate about it. These are two elements that need to meet.

If you find yourself doing something well, but no much love about it, then know that you will be good at it but never great. Unfortunately, this is the situation that most are living in.

But if you are passionate at something that you are not very good at, then it is a matter of time you will be great. Because passion will force you to keep learning about it. I see Cristiano Ronaldo on this point.

If it happens you have a natural talent at something

and you also have passion in it, then results will be magnificent. This is where Lionel Messi is.

But note that hard work beats talent when talent fails to work hard. Which means that even if you are talented, you still have to work hard to achieve great results.

Many people die with their raw talents because of fear of failure. They are forced to conform to the norms while their talents require the new environment to blossom. Fear of being uncommon, being different from the cloud accounts for most raw talents in the graveyard.

My take is that, if you want to leave a mark in this world you have to find your talent and your passion. These will bring a lot of happiness in your life and later money. But in the end, happiness is more important than money.

In every person, there is a hidden talent. Waiting to be uncovered polished and developed. When that is done, it can produce a lot of value.

41

Laugh Out Loud

I associate laughter with happiness. Laughing by itself has a lot of health benefits. Health specialists say it reduces stress hormones in your blood system, helps to control high blood pressure, and increases health-enhancing hormones, increases blood flow and so increase the amount of oxygen in the body. Also laughing helps your brain function much better and improve your memory.

So my friend when you get an opportunity to laugh, laugh, laugh long, laugh hard, and laugh out loud.

Laughter comes when you see or hear something that you feel is funny. So, in this case, I want you to look at laughter as a product of happiness, love and good living.

Human beings are social creatures. We are naturally wired to feel good and safe when we are in a company of others. I guess that is why we maintain family ties, clans, tribes and nations. That sense of belonging is part of our DNA. It makes us feel good.

Therefore it is important for you to appreciate the importance of community life and how best to live in order to be happy and grow love and happiness to others.

While we have talked about a lot of life skills that you need to acquire to bring success into your life, there are other simple acts that will keep the inner fire burning.

Others say, count your blessings. I say celebrate your achievements. However small the achievement might look, be happy about it. Sometimes by a simple act of punching your hand in the air, screaming, Yeeeah!, or a Hi Five!, or treating yourself with your favorite drink or cuisine. These simple acts boost your energy and passion.

Have you ever asked yourself why footballers and other players for that matter celebrate like crazy when they score a goal while the match has not ended yet? It is psychological. Celebrations raise their morale. You can do this too. Start celebrating your little achievements. Do it like no one is watching!

It is also nice to celebrate other people's achievements. It is an act of kindness and love. When friends do well, congratulate them. Call friends together and enjoy the moment. That is a good living.

In his famous book, Things Fall Apart, Chinua Achebe said, "A man who calls his kinsmen to a feast does not do so to save them from starving. They all have food in their own homes. When we gather together in the moonlit village ground it is not because of the moon. Every man can see it in his own compound. We come together because it is good for kinsmen to do so."

Now, if you want to be happy, do not turn up for a party or visit a good friend with your hands in the pocket. I mean, empty handed. That's very low. Grow up out of that. Carry a gift. Even in Holly Books it is written, "it better to give that to receive". It sounds ironic, but that is how it is. Gifts strengthen relationship bonds with family and friends. It shows that you care.

So when friends bring you gifts, be thankful. However small the gift might be. It does not matter. It simply means they care. Every gift should be valued on its own, do not compare with others. Giving gifts is a habit, develop it. It always puts a smile on your friend's faces.

It is said that when we grow old, things we will remember the most will be happy moments of our youth time. We will be telling our grandchildren stories of our happy times. That means what? It simply means you need to go out there and create those memorable moments. Pursue your hobbies.

What are your hobbies? Do you have any? You must have. I have not met anyone with no hobbies. Hobbies vary. To some their hobby could be cooking, drawing, painting, video games, cycling, swimming, engage in a sport or dancing.

My brother, Audax, who is an accomplished computer engineer, likes photographing so much. You can be sure at any event, party or journey he will be carrying his big camera. I am amazed by his love of photography.

I love watching sports like football, athletics and the like, but my love for books takes a larger chunk of my free time.

My simple message to you is while you chase success in our vision and goals, you have to know that true success comes when you are happy. And happiness can be found in your daily life through simple acts.

Others say, count your blessings. I say celebrate your achievements. However small the achievement might look, be happy about it.

42

Howl Like A Wolf

I know you are not a wolf and so it will be hard to howl exactly like a wolf. But you can try. Do you even know how a wolf howls? Find out. I find it fascinating.
Of recent, I have come to like wolves. Not because of how they are. Nothing fancy about their physical appearance. But I like wolves for their organizational skills. The way they have programmed their jungle life so that they can survive and thrive. They have a hierarchy of power. Each member of a pack knows where he belongs and the Alpha leads the pack. The most amazing thing about wolves is their howl. Howling is their main communication tool. When wolves howl they could be assembling their pack, claiming territory or warning intruders to keep away or just checking out if there are pack members in the area. The better communication is in the pack the more successful the pack will be.

So the success of the pack is in the howling.

Have you tried to howl already? Funny!

What howling is to wolves, so is speaking to humans. I mean people. You and me. Please note there is a difference between talking and speaking. At this point I know you must be able to talk unless you have a disability, but can you speak.

Leaders speak. Speaking is stronger and formal, talking is casual. Your ability to speak will always put you a step ahead of the pack. You will become the alpha wolf of your group.

I remember while in standard three, I was chosen to become a class monitor. I declined. My classmates assumed because I was doing well in my studies, I could also do well as a class monitor. They were wrong. I cried and the teacher picked another student. What a shame!

Come to think of it deeply, I declined because I couldn't gather enough courage to speak to my classmates. They were friends; I talked to them all the time, but the idea of speaking to them sent chills down my spine.

Fear of speaking in public is common to all human beings. It is normal. However, those who seem not to have it, are those who have learned how to overcome it. They have practices and managed to put that fear under control.

In my working life, I have seen many people either knowingly or unknowingly let pass their career growth opportunities because of their fear to speak. The way I was smart in my class but declined to take up the leadership of my class, it is the same way these young, smart professional fail to climb the corporate ladder. Their lack of confidence sabotages them.

Now I don't want you to go down the same road. Imagine after working hard in your studies, spent all those years in schools and colleges, pass the interview and mastering your responsibilities and now you are about to be promoted to your dream position only to be by the past because you can't stand up and speak. No, that is too painful. Don't sabotage your success.

Start today. Start now. How do you do that?

Start taking up duties that will require you to stand in front of your friends and speak. Be it a class monitor, prefect, project leader or sports captain. You can also volunteer to lead a class discussion on any matter. Take any role that will demand you to speak in front of others.

It is that simple. Practice, practice, practice.

The most important quality of a leader is the ability to communicate. Excellence in your career will take you so far, but your ability to communicate will open doors for leadership positions. And that is where the money is.

Look at people like Julius Nyerere, Nelson Mandela, and Kwame Nkrumah. These are great Africa leaders who are still remembered. I am not sure if they were the smartest of all, but I am sure they were the bravest; they had the courage to stand up, speak and lead tough movements.

Do you remember Barack Obama? He took America by storm and conquered the world by his speeches.

Thank me later, but now stand up and speak!

———————

Your ability to speak will always put you a step ahead of the pack. You will become the alpha wolf of your group.

———————

43

The Spirit of Charity

Now, this is a subject that is very close to my heart. A few days back I was driving from the airport. I had just picked my daughter, Nyakato, arriving from Mbeya for her semiannual leave. As we were talking, trying to catch up with each other she asked whether I was still in Rotary and she wanted to know when was the Rotary Dar Marathon coming up. I smiled and assured her that I am still a Rotarian and the marathon will be on October 14 as usual. She was sad that she could not attend because by that time she will be in school. She told me how she misses the Rotary events.

This conversation lasted for about three to five minutes but it has remained with me for weeks now. It has kept me thinking. I now realize how important it was introducing my twins, Nyakato and Ishengoma, to charity events. I knew they loved it, but I never realized how much impact it had in their lives.

— *Ntangeki Nshala* —

Now I might not have enough time to make you understand about Rotary International and the Rotary Dar Marathon, but the point here is the spirit of charity.

Charity is about helping those who are in need. Sharing our time, skills, money or things with those who are less privileged than us. By now I am sure you must have met people who need help. People who are in not able to help themselves out of their problems.

There are countless reasons why people find themselves in a situation where they need help. It could be because of lack of financial ability or sometimes it is because of emergencies like accidents.

It is common these days to hear about natural disasters like hurricanes, tsunami, floods or earthquakes. Sometimes it is war conflicts that cause people to leave their homes.

This simply means that any person, you and me, can find themselves in need of another person's help.

Therefore charity is about helping people you do not know, people from whom you do not expect to receive a payback. Helping people because they are human beings and they are in a situation where they cannot help themselves. It is about helping total strangers. That is what charity is all about.

The Spirit of Charity

Like I said I introduced my children to charity already. Now I want to introduce this spirit of charity to you too.

To be charitable does not require you to be rich, or very wealthy. No. It only requires you to look at a person in need and put yourself in his situation and try to feel how he feels. If you allow your mind to make that shift, I am sure you will find ways to help. Like I said, you can share your time, skills, money or things, depending on the situation at hand.

In some schools, colleges, and communities there are clubs that engage in charitable activities. Join them. Do not feel those clubs are for the rich or for special people. Members are normal people like you who have already realized that as human beings we need to support one another as much as possible.

Some people think it is the work of the government to solve all problems that people face. It is not correct. You need to do something too.

J.F Kennedy, former president of America once said, "Do not ask what the country is going to do for you, ask yourself what you are going to do for your country."

Some charitable activities could be like visiting orphanages, hospitals, other schools, or other places that need help. But also you can look around in your own environment; there could be people in need.

I want you to grow up to a responsible citizen. Start now to build this important habit. The habit of volunteering for the benefit of others without expecting a pay. Actually the pay you might get is a, "Thank you." But there is a good feeling you get after helping people. That is the real pay.

So go out there, be charitable, volunteer and become a responsible citizen. Your reward will be greater than money.

Charity is about helping those who are in need. Sharing our time, skills, money or things with those who are less privileged than us.

44

Floor Your Flaws

I like watching boxing. I remember those days we had to spend sleepless nights to watch Mike Tyson fights. We would spend the whole evening discussing how fascinating the event would be. Only to watch one round or if very lucky, two rounds and the fight is over. Mike Tyson would floor his opponents in just a few minutes.

This is what I want you to do too. I want you to floor your flaws.

No one is perfect. Not me may be not you. Every human being has his own problems.

However, all successful people strive to perfect themselves. They want to fight their flaws, bad habits which make them imperfect. They have already realized that these bad habits might become stumbling blocks to their success. So they engage in a constant fight until they floor their opponents, their bad habits, their flaws.

Now you might want to search for your life and see what could be your bad habits that you need to fight until you win. Fight until you knock them to the floor.

Habits become bad if they are not acceptable to the community, according to your culture. But there are some that are universal, especially for youth. The list might include taking alcoholic drinks, smoking, drugs, too much social media, pre-marital relationships, obsession with junk foods, use of bad language, lack of respect to elders, time wasting activities, laziness and so on.

But it is up to you to identify habits that you feel you are not comfortable with so that you can find ways of fighting them.

Most of the time bad habits are nice to do. Our minds have already loved them, may be because we have engaged in them for a long time. That is why the wise said, bad habits die hard.

Now, Mike Tyson used to floor his opponents very easily. But you can also remember that he could not floor his bad habits and they made him go to jail. Fighting a person in a ring requires physical strength while fighting

Floor Your Flaws

a bad habit required mental strength.

You will require strong determination, discipline, and patience to win against an established bad habit. It will take time. You have to have a plan, and techniques to effectively execute it.

I recommend three steps to help you overcome your unwanted habits;

First, you need to list all of them down and put down. This will help you get a clear picture of much work you need to do to overcome them.

Second; for each bad habit, find a good habit to replace it. Like the time you used in a pub drinking, what activity will occupy that space? Is it reading, jogging or working? Whatever it may be, find a substitute.

Third; involve a trusted friend about your plans so that he can help as a controller to remind you whenever you are tempted to slip back.

You can also find your own suitable methods that will help you overcome and floor these future obstacles towards your success.

Don't rest until you have floored all your flaws. Be vigilant and mindful all the time. Always remember that success comes to the real fighters.

Wish you a good fight!

You will require strong determination, discipline, and patience to win against an established bad habit. It will take time. You have to have a plan, and techniques to effectively execute it.

45

Excellence

Excellence is a habit. It is a habit of performing at expected standards. Highest standards possible. Actually, excellence is not a skill, but an attitude. It is not something you are going to be taught to do. It is a mental position that one takes, to always carry any undertaking to the best of his or her ability.

Since it is an attitude, it will affect all aspects of yours. When you attain that mental attitude, you will always know the quality of the product of your work before you begin, and by the time you finish you will know whether you have the expected product or not. You have to be very honest with yourself. Your answers should always be yes or no. Is this the expected standard or not? Do not allow "if"s and "but"s. It is a black or white answer, no gray.

When you meet excellence you will know it, and when you meet mediocrity you will know it too.

A few years back, there was a very publicized blunder done by doctors in a hospital where they operated a patient on his head instead of his foot, and to another one, they operated a foot instead of his head. The simple excuse was the confusion on the names. Just like that. Now that is what I call mediocrity. Mediocre doctors giving a mediocre performance.

If you open your eyes, you will see a lot of lack of excellence in many areas. Every day we pass on roads which are constructed using billions of money, but after a short time, the same roads are full of potholes. If you look at the qualifications of all those involved in these works you will be amazed. They all seem to be highly qualified with nice university grades. They look super on paper, mediocre in performance.

Remember I said excellence is not a skill, it is an attitude. If it were a skill, then these best doctors and engineers would be producing super results. But it is not the case. They have a wrong attitude.

These professionals do not care about the quality of their service. They just work to make money and go. It is a shame.

Excellence

This is exactly why I am writing this to you. So that you know from early on that if you want success in your life there are some simple qualities you will need to develop. These are never taught in school, excellence being one of them.

People, who are not ready to push themselves for excellence, are the majority who always wonder why they do not make it in life. Their work barely meets the minimum standards not to be fired. Their lives end up to be hand to mouth. These can easily succumb to corruption and other shoddy behaviors.

So what should you do to develop this attitude? I will recommend a few steps;

Set standards – for whatever you do in all aspects of your life have standards. Then always work to meet them and then beat them and then set new standards. This way you will keep improving and stand out of the crowd.

Role model – look at the best in the industry or area and work to be like them. Role models are meant to inspire you and affirm that it is possible because someone already has done it.

Strategy – once you have set the standard, then you will have a strategy to achieve it. Do not expect things to happen, nothing happens until someone does something. Plan and execute.

Work hard – now this goes without saying. You will not achieve extraordinary results without putting extraordinary efforts. Never. Hard work, long hours is a constant in any equation of success.

In conclusion, I need you to trust what I am advising you here, because this is how I operate and it has never failed me. So I want you to go out there and start working on all these. The fact is, real sustainable success will not come without embracing excellence in whatever you do. Start now.

Actually, excellence is not a skill, but an attitude. It is not something you are going to be taught to do. It is a mental position that one takes, to always carry any undertaking to the best of his or her ability.

46

Be Like MJ

Yes, be like Michael Jordan. The legendary basketball superstar. We all know him very well as one of all time super talented player who broke many records and won many personal achievements awards in the USA Basketball League, the NBA. But that is not all, when he was in high school he was deemed not good enough to play for the senior team. He says that he cried a lot, for being dropped, but he was determined to make it. He later did, and the rest is history.

Look at what MJ did after he got dropped. He was very disappointed. But did not lose focus of playing in the senior team. He took it as a challenge. He did not despair. Instead, he doubled the effort, he trained even harder.

His attitude is what helped him. This is a big lesson.

He did not allow another person's opinion define his destiny.

Dr. Myles Munroe, one of the finest leadership and personal development gurus from The Bahamas, gave his story. He said when he was growing up in the poor neighborhood, one of his school teachers told him that he was mentally retarded and so unable to learn. He said that statement hurt him. However, he did not agree with that prejudiced teacher's opinion. He went on to become a world-class leadership expert and went around the world training many leaders. He also authored many bestselling books.

His teacher misjudged him, maybe because he was from a very poor family. Instead of helping him learn, he judged him. He was wrong. Although Dr. Myles Munroe has passed on, his books will be used for many years to come.

These two scenarios are a clear indication that people might judge you. They might discourage you. They might even call you crazy. But never leave your course because of other people's opinion.

As long as you are sure of what you want to achieve, keep moving.

Be like MJ

Many times people discourage others, because they failed, or they do not have enough courage to start, so they want you to be like them.

There is one old adage which says, "Those who danced were thought to be insane by those who couldn't hear the music." You see!

Sometimes people discourage you because they have no idea of where you are heading to. Keep moving. Follow your dream.

When a teacher or any other person tells you that you cannot, stay focused, work hard to prove them wrong. In school or college, there are subjects which will be a bit harder for you, but let me tell you this. Nothing can stop a determined mind. If you put your mind on a subject, and a spend time on it, nothing is impossible. I have experienced it myself. So I know.

Things only become difficult because we go into them with divided attention, with no deep determination to win. Sometimes we want quick results, but the reality is always different. There is no overnight success.

Life has never been a straight line or a smooth road. There are obstacles and ups and downs. All great achievements come out of perseverance.

Dale Carnegie once said, "Most of the important things in the world have been accomplished by people who have kept on trying when there seemed to be no hope at all."

If I were to borrow the words of Christopher Robin, then I would like to conclude by telling you that please, Promise me you'll always remember that: You're braver than you believe and stronger than you seem, and smarter than you think.

Most of the important things in the world have been accomplished by people who have kept on trying when there seemed to be no hope at all." – Dale Carnegie, (an American Writer) -

---

47

Keep Your Word

Honor all your promise however difficult, expensive or inconvenient it may be. As long as you made the promise, there is no going back; lest you lose your trust. Are we together? A simple rule, never make promises you cannot honor, and honor all promises you make. Your word should have the highest value. You should always say what you mean, and mean what you say.

I once worked with a leader who would come to a meeting and promise several benefits to staff. However, after some time when people remind him about the promises, he becomes furious and never fulfilled them. After sometime staff lost trust in him and became very demoralized.

Trust is what makes our society function. In the business world, there are many legal contracts. But all these came after people falling to keep their words. However, even those legal contracts still need trust to work; otherwise, it will be war everywhere. Who will sign a legal contract with a person he knows will not honor it. No one.

It is said the greatest punishment you can give a person who is not trustworthy is, not believing him even when he says the truth.

I am sure you do not want to be in a position like this. Where whatever you say people have to double check before believing in it.

Keeping your word starts with fulfilling your own goals. Doing what you promised yourself. If you push yourself to accomplish your personal promises, you will find yourself compelled to fulfill the promise you made to others. Make your word sacred.

Keeping your word is the essence of integrity. A person of integrity matches his actions with his words.

John Maxwell said leadership is influence. So if you need to have influence over others you have to be trustworthy.

I find a person who does not keep his word to be disrespectful too. It means he thinks people are not worthy the truth. They can be lied to and nothing will happen. It is arrogance.

Keep Your Word

Of course, if you do not keep your word, your respect among your people vanishes. Your value goes down.

Now, you might be thinking that these do not apply to you. They do. Promises do not have to be bid or expensive things. I am talking about your everyday life. Whether in school, college, at work or at home. However small a promise might be, just fulfill it. Because you will not fulfill a big promise if you fail to fulfill a small one.

If you made a commitment to wake up at 5:00 am, then wake up at 5:00 am. If you promised to always be punctual, then be on time no matter what. If you promised to work hard, then work hard. If you make a commitment to always be honest and say the truth, do so no matter what. Don't fail yourself.

Simple things can reflect negatively on you, like promising to call back, and you do not.

It is important to understand the importance of these qualities now so that you slowly develop them for your future.

Trust, honesty and integrity and the like are corner stones for success. If you cannot be trusted, then you will not accomplish much however talented you might be. No amount of resources and hard work will bring

Ntangeki Nshala

you success in the absence of trust.

So keep your word, build trust and live with integrity.

Your word should have the highest value. You should always say what you mean, and mean what you say.

48

Be Humble

Humbleness is felt when others see you as modest, ordinary, maintaining reasonable relation with people around you, despite extraordinary success.

A humble person's success is valuable only when it enables him or her to become a better person in the community. Humble people are those who have succeeded in detaching themselves from their positions, titles and wealth and still consider themselves as a work in progress like any other person across a street.

Humble people, although very successful in their areas, don't view themselves as being special, better than others or even smarter. Although other people may see them as special, genius or superstars they are happy about it but don't allow to be carried away by praises.

That is how people are expected to behave. Rational people are humble people. Football fans can remember when Jose' Mourinho was recruited to coach Chelsea FC in the English Premier League he said he was the 'special one.' That statement never went down well with many fans, although Mourinho has been a great coach. But the fact that he considers himself 'special' it is an indication of arrogance.

An arrogant person is not humble. He feels he is better than others and looks down on his peers. Arrogant people brag around because of their achievements. Naturally, that turns other people away from them. They have very few or no true friends.

Julius Nyerere, the first President of Tanzania, is an icon of a humble person. He was the leader of the country for more than two decades but led a simple life. When he voluntarily retired, he went to live in his village to live a normal life, in a very modest house. He was the most powerful person in the country, during and after his presidency, he was adored by many and respected by all, but he considered himself a loyal servant of all.

 Humble people do not attach themselves with things or situations. They are above things, titles, privileges, and praises. They can live very well with them, but also they

— Be Humble —

can still enjoy their lives without them. Humble people can let go easily.

Letting go is when you are compelled to leave a place, things or people. It is normally a painful process to let go of a thing, place or people you loved. But sometimes situations demand changes, and you find yourself having to let go. When our friends leave us, we cry. Some get sick because their title has been removed. Some commit suicide because they became bankrupt. Somehow somewhere you are bound to find yourself in such a situation. Let go! It is nice to have good things, but don't kill yourself when they are no longer available. Things shouldn't define you. That is humbleness.

Humble people don't hold grudges. They know life is too short to waste it on useless personal wars. Life is about happiness. People might hurt you but allow healing to take place. Forgive, forget and move on. To err is human. No one is perfect. Eye for an eye will leave all people blind. Humble people do not take things too personal. I want you to understand this too. If Nelson Mandela forgave people who jailed and tortured him for 27 years, what is it that prevents you to forgive?

Above all, humble people are respectful people. A humble person might be so good at a certain subject but will allow others to express their views, even when he does not agree with their position. A humble person seeks to learn from others. He listens. He does not claim to know all. However accomplished he or she might be, she still knows there is a room for improvement.

If you want to have a good life you have to learn to be humble. You have to start now. It will be too late to wait until you are super rich, or successful in your career to start to be humble. As a matter of fact, the lack of it or presence of arrogance might limit your success.

Humble people, although very successful in their areas, don't view themselves as being special, better than others or even smarter.

49

A Valuable Brand

It might be the first time you meet this word, 'brand." Do not worry. It is a simple but confusing concept. Even some professionals struggle with it. I will make is as simple as possible.

My definition is that a brand is a unique perception, feeling or emotion that is attached to a name. What do you think or feel when you hear Coca-cola, Kilimanjaro Drinking Water, Safari Beer, Clouds FM, Julius Nyerere, Nelson Mandela, or Diamond Platnumz.

There are many products that you know. Those that you love, value most because of their quality are brands and those that you do not care or know much about are commodities.

Are we still together?

A customer or a user is the one who determines which product is a brand and which one is a commodity.

What comes to your mind when you read; St. Francis Girls Secondary School, Marian, Feza, Canossa or Libermann or maybe Oxford University, Harvard, Yale, or University of Dar es Salaam.

Your feeling about these products is the value you place on their names. If it is a positive feeling then it is a good brand, if it is neutral then it is a commodity or if it is bad then it is a bad brand.

I believe we are still together up to this point. I know the brand concept is simple but sometimes confusing.

Now see, commodities are shopped for their price, but brands are acquired for their value. People will buy the cheapest commodity because it just saves the purpose. But the same people are ready to pay more for a brand even if it saves the same purpose as a commodity.

There are many secondary schools around but people will pay more to go to Feza, Marian, Canossa, St. Francis or Libermann. This world has millions of universities but people will pay a fortune to go to Harvard. Why? It is the brand. The perceived quality of education in those schools. Simple and clear.

A Valuable Brand

Now, why am I taking you through this branding journey? I have a good reason. The world has more than 6 billion people now. You do not have to be an economist to know that resources or opportunities are few and only the best will get them.

I have written this book for this single reason; to make you competitive in the world full of tough competitions. The whole 50 lessons I am giving you are intended to help you at this early age to know and prepare for a tough life ahead.

You have to make yourself a brand to all who know you. You have to have a differentiating factor. That differentiating factor has to be of high quality and above all be known to people.

There will be many accountants, doctors, lawyers, musicians, teachers, engineers, and so on, but what will make you stand out. You will have to make yourself more valuable than your peers otherwise you will be lost in the crowd.

There are many musicians but Diamond Platnumz stands out. Many footballers but Christiano Ronaldo and Messi are special. They play in their teams but they are the most paid.

Ntangeki Nshala

You have to be special in your field or career to be a powerful brand and that is how you will succeed.

Turn yourself into a valuable brand and take good care of yourself and success will follow you.

Now see, commodities are shopped for their price, but brands are acquired for their value.

50

It's Show Time

At this point, I assume we have been together from other previous lessons. I believe I was able to make you learn some new ideas or make those that you already knew clearer. It has been a long journey of discovery, soul searching, determination and decision making.

Some concepts may not be clear to you if you meet them for the first time, but I expect you to read this book several times. This is how I do too. Experience has shown me that some lessons open up during the third or fourth reading. The first time you read a book you think you got it all, but when you go back the second time you gather something new. That is why I like reading my books slowly, page by page, chapter by chapter, because am in no hurry.

You may wish to try this too. Don't rush. According to your time, you may read a chapter and give yourself time to meditate on it and see how you can absorb it in your situation.

This is not an academic book that you read to pass your exam. Here, you are reading for your own personal development. Because if you don't understand, then you will not manage to put it into practice.

I want you now to go out there and put all that you have learned from here into action. Show yourself that you have changed because of what you learned here. Show your friends that you are no longer the same. Show your parents that buying and reading this book was worthwhile.

Let me give you this. Most people, all over the world, are struggling with their lives not because they are not educated, not because they have never heard the principles of success, and not because they do not know what to do to succeed in life. Not at all! They have what is takes to succeed and they know what to do to succeed. Now, what is their problem? Their problem is that they do not put into practice what they know.

Do not be like them. Don't be lazy. Be as hungry as a wolf. Create an unquenchable thirst for success.

— *It's Show Time* —

I believe your age is the right age to start acquiring these very valuable lessons that no school teaches. While you need to do well in school, my lessons will make you produce extraordinary results in school and in life.

While my lessons are simple, they are not easy to internalize. But that is why I have decided to give you these lessons now, at a young age, while most people get them while they are already grown up adults.

Without practice, all that I have put down for you will amount to nothing. That is not my intention. My intention is to help you meet me at the top.

So, go out there, learn and practice, then learn and practice and learn and practice and then show the whole world the best of you.

Remember, if it has to be, it is up to you!

Without practice, all that I have put down for you will amount to nothing. That is never my intention. My intention is to help you meet me at the top.

HOMEWORK

"You have to make your own condensed notes. You learn from MAKING them. A lot of thinking goes into deciding what to include and exclude. You develop your own system of abbreviations and memory methods for the information."
◆ Peter Rogers, Straight A at Stanford and on to Harvard

I. Chapter Summary

1. Note down a summary of Chapter One – Born to Lead

   ....
   ....
   ....

2. Note down a summary of Chapter Two – Fear of God

   ....
   ....
   ....

3. Note down a summary of Chapter Three –Dream Big

....

....

....

4. Note down a summary of Chapter Four – Parent's Pride

....

....

....

5. Note down a summary of Chapter Five –Finish Your Greens

....

....

....

6. Note down a summary of Chapter Six – Home Alone

....

....

....

7. Note down a summary of Chapter Seven – Smart & Clean

....

....

....

8. Note down a summary of Chapter Eight – Eagles Flock with Eagles

....

....

....

9. Note down a summary of Chapter Nine – Read a Lot

....

....

....

10. Note down a summary of Chapter Ten – Sit in Front

....

....

....

11. Note down a summary of Chapter Eleven – Volunteer to Lead

   ....
   ....
   ....

12. Note down a summary of Chapter Twelve – Family First

   ....
   ....
   ....

13. Note down a summary of Chapter Thirteen – Fear Fear!

   ....
   ....
   ....

14. Note down a summary of Chapter Fourteen – Time is Precious

   ....
   ....
   ....

15. Note down a summary of Chapter Fifteen – Peer Pressure

....

....

....

16. Note down a summary of Chapter Sixteen – Girls Power

....

....

....

17. Note down a summary of Chapter Seventeen - Boys to Men

....

....

....

18. Note down a summary of Chapter Eighteen – Truth will Set You Free

....

....

....

— Homework —

19. Note down a summary of Chapter Nineteen – Devil's Workshop

....
....
....

20. Note down a summary of Chapter Twenty – Work Hard

....
....
....

21. Note down a summary of Chapter Twenty One – A Myth of a Private Life

....
....
....

22. Note down a summary of Chapter Twenty Two – Hired for Attitude

....
....
....

23. Note down a summary of Chapter Twenty Three – Sky is Never the Limit

....

....

....

24. Note down a summary of Chapter Twenty Four – Never Lose Your Cool

....

....

....

25. Note down a summary of Chapter Twenty Five – Think

....

....

....

26. Note down a summary of Chapter Twenty Six – Critical Thinking

....

....

....

27. Note down a summary of Chapter Twenty Seven – Dig Gold where You Are

....

....

....

28. Note down a summary of Chapter Twenty Eight – Biija Mpola

....

....

....

29. Note down a summary of Chapter Twenty Nine – In Rome, Be a Roman

....

....

....

30. Note down a summary of Chapter Thirty – Education is Key

....

....

....

31. Note down a summary of Chapter Thirty One – Talent is Never Enough

....

....

....

32. Note down a summary of Chapter Thirty Two – Kindness Matters

....

....

....

33. Note down a summary of Chapter Thirty Three – Exercise is Power

....

....

....

34. Note down a summary of Chapter Thirty Four – Live Legally

....

....

....

— Homework —

35. Note down a summary of Chapter Thirty Five
    – Set Goals

    ....
    ....
    ....

36. Note down a summary of Chapter Thirty Six –
    Fluent in Finance

    ....
    ....
    ....

37. Note down a summary of Chapter Thirty Seven
    – A Wolf in a Pack

    ....
    ....
    ....

38. Note down a summary of Chapter Thirty Eight –
    The Power of Words

    ....
    ....
    ....

39. Note down a summary of Chapter Thirty Nine – Who is Your Role Model

....

....

....

40. Note down a summary of Chapter Forty – A Drop of Greatness

....

....

....

41. Note down a summary of Chapter Forty One – Laugh Out Loud

....

....

....

42. Note down a summary of Chapter Forty Two – Howl Like a Wolf

....

....

....

43. Note down a summary of Chapter Forty Three – The Spirit of Charity

....

....

....

44. Note down a summary of Chapter Forty Four – Floor Your Flaws

....

....

....

45. Note down a summary of Chapter Forty Five – Excellence

....

....

....

46. Note down a summary of Chapter Forty Six – Be Like MJ

....

....

....

47. Note down a summary of Chapter Forty Seven – Keep Your Word

....

....

....

48. Note down a summary of Chapter Forty Eight – Humble

....

....

....

49. Note down a summary of Chapter Forty Nine – A Valuable Brand

....

....

....

50. Note down a summary of Chapter Fifty – It's Show Time

....

....

....

— *Homework* —

II. Which Chapter did you like the most? (Give reasons)

....

....

....

III. Write down your Vision statement (in 20 words or less)

To be...

....

....

IV. Write down names of your three role models

    1..

    2..

    3..

V. Write down your top three goals for this year.

    Goal 1…………………………………………….

    Goal 2…………………………………………….

    Goal 3…………………………………………….

VI. Write down three actions your will take to accomplish Goal 1

    1…………………………………………………..

    2…………………………………………………..

    3…………………………………………………..

VII. Write down three actions your will take to accomplish Goal 2

    1…………………………………………………..

    2…………………………………………………..

    3…………………………………………………..

— *Homework* —

VIII. Write down three actions your will take to accomplish Goal 3

    1..

    2..

    3..

IX. List down three habits that you are going to change/improve this year.

    1..

    2..

    3..

x. Who is going to be your accountability partner (a trusted person you will share these goals with so that he/she can watch and remind you to stay on track)

....

NOTES

Notes

Notes

www.ingramcontent.com/pod-product-compliance
Lightning Source LLC
Chambersburg PA
CBHW032032040426
42449CB00007B/859